Connected for All Time

Book One

A Spiritual Solution to Grief
After Miscarriage or Infant Loss

Sharon J. Wesch, Ph.D.

Copyright © 2023 by Sharon J. Wesch, Ph.D.
ISBN 978-0-9839173-0-4
Second Printing

Cover Artwork: Carolyn Utigard Thomas (www.utigard.com)
Layout and design: Kouba Graphics, Inc. (www.koubagraphics.com)

10 9 8 7 6 5 4 3

Dedication

This book is dedicated to all the
spirit babies in these stories.
They bring powerful medicine
for healing grief.

Angel's Lullaby

By Carolyn Utigard Thomas
(www.utigard.com)

This guardian angel embraces an infant
in everlasting peace and safety.
Be comforted by her loving gaze
and listen for her quiet lullaby.

Table of Contents

Table of Contents

Introduction

Deep grief after the tragedy of a miscarriage, a stillbirth, or the death of a beloved infant sometimes progresses into an all-encompassing feeling of spiritual disconnection—what I call a wounding to the soul, or soul loss. If you've experienced such a misfortune, a piece of your soul is missing and must be reclaimed or reconnected before you can feel whole again. After soul loss, you may have found yourself thinking, "I feel alone, lost, and isolated from everybody, including God. There's an empty place in my heart that can never be filled." These are the everyday, normal thoughts of people who have not yet found a way to heal their soul loss after the tragedy of infant death.

This book will show you how to heal your soul wound. It doesn't matter if you miscarried within days after conception, birthed a full-term stillborn baby, or lost your beloved baby months after childbirth. *You can heal your grief.* Also, it doesn't matter if you've been in grief for a few weeks, a few months, or many, many years. *It's never too late to heal.*

While traditional psychotherapy, commonly called grief counseling, or "talk therapy," can help you find numerous ways to cope with grief, it cannot heal the deep anguish that sears your soul after infant death. It's an impossible expectation. I know because I'm a trained psychotherapist with a doctorate in clinical psychology and thirty years of experience working with bereaved clients. This work, as well as my own journey through grief, has taught me that a soul wound demands something different. It demands a spiritual solution—a way of satisfying the deep longing for connection with the spirit of your deceased loved one. *The purpose of this book is to provide that spiritual solution.*

Connected for All Time: Book One presents that solution through storytelling, an ancient way of teaching. It's a marvelous means of sharing wisdom because stories can open your heart, touch your soul, and provide hope for healing. This collection of sacred stories from ordinary people demonstrates again and again that recognizing signs and messages from your spirit baby opens your heart to the healing power of spiritual connection. The many mystical experiences of grieving loved ones in this book are a testament to the healing power of the spirit babies. The soul love they send through the veil is the most powerful medicine for healing your broken heart. *The key is learning to open your heart and feel this love.*

What You'll Find in This Book

Connected for All Time: Book One is divided into three sections. In Part I you'll find many beautiful love stories portraying soul love as a powerful force that reaches across time and space. These five chapters will help you:

1) Learn about the ancient traditions of the Inca people when a baby dies—they know the healing power of the spirit babies.

2) Recognize the twelve different ways spirit babies send signs and messages.

3) Invoke the assistance of angels and ask them to help you with your journey through grief.

4) Identify visitation dreams and interpret them so healing occurs.

5) Realize that the bonds of family love stretch into eternity and are never broken.

In Part II you'll find a step-by-step method for creating a spiritual solution to your grief. This section offers you an easy-to-follow map for healing your soul wound; it includes proven self-healing tools that are simple to learn, easy to use, and give you practical techniques to speed up your healing journey. More true stories show you it's possible to completely free yourself from suffering and to transform your grief into the joy of spiritual connection.

You will also find my unique way of defining grief—it is a heavy, crushing energy that fills the cells of your body. It collects mainly in your heart area, causing a feeling of pressure in your chest. Radiant Heart Healing, a spiritual process I created, uses simple visualizations to remove this oppressive energy from your heart. This method of healing is my life's work, and I've used it effectively to alleviate grief for the past thirty years. *The goal of Radiant Heart Healing is to remember your baby with love instead of pain.*

Part III contains three stories, each one describing the spiritual transformation of a grief stricken mother as she heals her soul loss after the death of a beloved infant. Each mother finds herself awakening to Spirit through the wondrous gift of connecting to a precious spirit baby. This awakening is the most important goal of our soul journey here on earth. These inspirational stories—each one unique—contain profound wisdom.

Challenging Old Paradigms

My goal in this book is to gently lead you down a new path, a path perhaps different from the norm. These fascinating stories of mystical experiences are meant to open your heart to the love coming from your spirit baby and to open your mind to new beliefs. Once you've freed both your heart and your mind, you are more likely to have an experience of spiritual connection. Then you will be comfortable with these evolutionary concepts and see them as valid:

- My baby is a powerful, eternal soul, as am I.
- Spirit babies send powerful medicine and act as healers for the family.
- Our precious baby came to our family to awaken me to the truth of who I really am.
- Everything that happened was meant to be and had a spiritual purpose.

PREFACE

My Journey of Spiritual Awakening

With each life challenge you have the opportunity to create a defining moment—a time when you make a choice to follow your heart and take a different path—different from any you've ever taken before, and different from the norm. These choices will define who you become.

As a young adult, I had no plans to become an expert in grief psychotherapy or to write a book about using spirit communication to assist in healing grief after the loss of an infant. In fact, until age forty, I didn't even believe in spirit communication.

However, when you follow your heart and listen to the small whispering voice of your soul, you can end up on an adventurous, sometimes scary journey that takes you far beyond the conscious agenda you had for your life. "Following your heart and listening to your soul" is a pat phrase that may sound easy—believe me, it's not. My soul called for me to evolve, grow bigger, and transform myself in order to transcend the challenges in my life. This is always the way of the soul, though I didn't understand this for a long time.

There are three major challenges in my life that eventually led to my writing this book: my father's death (1974), my dear mother-in-law's transition (1982), and the death of a baby named Cole (2000). The theme of spiritual disconnection versus spiritual connection is present in all three events. With my father's death I experienced the all-encompassing feeling of spiritual disconnection that often accompanies deep grief. In contrast, eight years later, after my mother-in-law's death, a visitation from her spirit gifted me with a moment of deep connection. It was my spiritual awakening! Then, after Baby Cole's death, I helped his family members heal their grief by affirming the messages coming from their spirit baby. The choices I made regarding these events have taken me down a different path—different from any I'd ever taken before, and different from the norm. These choices have also defined who I have become—a spiritual healer and the author of grief books that are also quite different from the norm.

Feeling Disconnected

I was living an ordinary life in Indiana as a mathematics teacher, wife, and mother of two young children, ages five and four. Suddenly, it seemed God pulled the rug out from under me—my father had a massive heart attack. He was only fifty-seven, so young to have his life just end with no warning. At that time, my dad was the light of my life, my soul mate, and the most important source of love in my life. Consequently, my grief was overwhelming. I was in the depths of despair and even had daily suicidal thoughts. I remember thinking, *"The light has gone out of my life. Since he's not here I don't want to stay. I want to go be with him in heaven."* The only thing that kept me from acting on those thoughts was knowing my children needed a mother to take care of them. And so I stayed.

When my father died, my beliefs about life after death were not well defined. I believed the traditional religious teachings that said my father's spirit was now in heaven, but that idea brought me no solace. It seemed my father's spirit went into some dark place—a place I couldn't go. I wasn't aware of any signs or messages and had no sense that he was present and watching over me. All I had was a desperate longing to have him back on earth to light up my life once again. I yearned for a sense of connection to his spirit; yet, I could feel nothing. I felt alone, lost, and disconnected from everything, including God.

Weeks after my father's death, I made a decision to begin grief psychotherapy. This choice was one of those defining moments. At the time, this felt like a huge risk because just the word "therapy" brought feelings of shame and embarrassment. Being in therapy was something most people didn't want the neighbors to know, especially in small-town Midwestern America. In spite of my fears, I found that I loved learning about releasing painful emotions, identifying the victim patterns in my life, and becoming a more empowered person. Gradually, I realized I had to grow and transform myself—including how I looked at life—in order to alleviate my emotional pain. I found myself asking, *"Why didn't anyone teach me all of this earlier in life?"*

The next year was a time of great personal growth and change. The most important change was that I fell in love with the process of therapy—it became my passion. After alleviating my suicidal thoughts and my severe depression, I made a very unexpected life-changing decision. I enrolled in a doctoral program for clinical psychology; this path was certainly different from any I'd ever taken before and also different from the norm. Since I was not yet spiritually awake, I had no way of knowing my soul was nudging me to take this new direction. I was operating in the dark—still thinking I was in charge of my life.

The personal growth work I did in both my initial year of psychotherapy and my five years of training to become a therapist brought much relief for my grief, but neither process addressed my feeling of disconnection—*the wounding to my soul.* As is customary in traditional grief psychotherapy, my therapist, and later my professors, kept the process focused at the personality level, dealing with my feelings, thoughts, and behaviors, while avoiding any discussion about the spiritual aspects of life. Using this approach, I learned to manage my grief—to keep it under control—but I knew it wasn't truly healed because nothing seemed to soothe *the deep longing for connection with my father.* I remember thinking, *"Well, I guess this is as good as it gets. I'll just have to live with it. There's nothing else to do."*

Staying Connected

In 1982, eight years after my father's death, and just months after my fortieth birthday, Golda, my mother-in-law with whom I shared a deep mother-daughter love, died of cancer. Two days after her funeral, I had a mind-expanding experience when my dear, sweet Golda appeared in my living room. She was radiant and whole again; a spiritual light emanated from her heart as well as her face. Indeed, she had this magnificent glow about her that lit up the room. Using mental telepathy, Golda sent me this simple message, "I've come to say goodbye." Then she leaned forward, kissed me lightly on the cheek, and disappeared into thin air. Such a butterfly kiss! I didn't have time to feel scared—instead I was filled with wonder. It was an awesome moment!

Golda's visitation lasted all of five seconds, but I was forever changed. This experience transformed all my beliefs about life, death, and the afterlife. I didn't have to think about it and decide—I just knew these ideas to be true: *Life is eternal and spirit communication is real. Love continues and can pierce the veil between the two worlds. There is no death. My fear of death is gone.*

My mother-in-law's appearance also created a burning desire to understand this spiritual encounter. *How was I able to perceive my mother-in-law as a spirit? Why had I not had the same experience with my father? Was my father also alive and radiant somewhere in the universe? Why was I given this wonderful gift of connection? What was I to do with this gift?* I had so many questions and no answers. With great passion, I began reading everything I could find on life after death, spirit communication, and the spiritualist movement that was very active in the United States in the late 1800s. I fell in love once again—this time with learning about staying connected with our deceased loved ones in the afterlife.

After filling my library with every book published on this subject, I woke up one day and realized I was on a new path. This time it was a path that led even further away from the norm, but that was not a concern. I just kept following my heart. In quiet moments, I sometimes wonder how my life would have unfolded if Golda had not blessed me with her presence that day.

My investigation of paranormal research revealed that it's actually quite common for ordinary people to have experiences involving the appearance of deceased loved ones. In fact, fifty per cent of people acknowledge they have had some kind of mystical or psychic experience; however, most keep this a secret. All of this information silenced the doubting voice in my head: *Did Golda really appear or did I imagine it? Was it just a dream? Was I going crazy?* I still chose to keep Golda's visitation a secret even though I came to understand I wasn't crazy. At the time, I believed others might define me as such; hence my decision to remain in the closet about this awesome mystical experience.

Taking a Different Path

For many years, researching the afterlife was only my hobby; my major focus was completing my doctorate in psychology and then opening a holistic medical center where I lived in Indiana. While driving back and forth to the clinic, I sometimes found myself pondering my mystical experience with Golda. I also wondered about my dad's spirit: *Where is he now? Will I ever connect with him again? I know I'll see him when I get to heaven, but why doesn't he come like Golda did?*

There's a wise spiritual saying: "When the student is ready, the teacher appears." My desire to understand the spiritual aspects of life attracted many new teachers into my life. I met some of them while attending a week-long conference that offered classes on energy healing, psychic development, life after death, and spirit communication. I loved every minute of my conference time and was so excited about this new knowledge that I could hardly sleep. It truly fed my soul!

While at this conference, I decided to take a chance and sit for my first "reading" with a spiritual medium; these are people who have the ability to deliver messages from deceased loved ones. This turned out to be another choice that changed the course of my career and my life. At the time, it seemed like a "crazy" thing to do, but I followed my heart, shutting out the doubting voice in my head. The conference had a staff of twenty spiritual mediums; I randomly picked Roy Waite off a list and made an appointment for the following day. That night I went to sleep praying, "Dear Dad and Golda, please come talk to me through Roy Waite tomorrow."

Awakening very early the next morning, I decided to take a walk along the river that ran through the college campus where this conference was held. Watching the sunlight sparkle on the water and listening to the rush of the river put me in a quiet meditative state. Suddenly, beautiful music filled my whole being—like a host of angels was singing; then, the song "I Love You Truly" began playing in my head. Tears ran down my face as the words to all the verses flowed unbidden into my mind. This was an amazing experience because I didn't really know all the words to the song! My heart burst with a feeling of deep love that surrounded my whole being. It was like being wrapped in a soft blanket of pink love. My mind could make no sense of this experience—I could only feel it with my heart. My thoughts turned to my father, and I wondered if it could be him. Actually, I hoped this miraculous gift came from him, but I didn't trust my intuition enough to really believe it could be true.

Hours later I nervously joined Roy for my reading. We sat on wooden classroom chairs facing each other in a small, sparsely furnished college dormitory room. My heart pounded so hard I could barely hear. Roy described three powerful guides who continually surround me, bringing me inspiration to keep moving forward on my path of spiritual enlightenment. This was a complete surprise to me, but I accepted it as truth. Then, before I could catch my breath he announced:

> *There's the spirit of a man standing behind you with his hand on your shoulder. Can you feel him? (No.) He must have died of a heart attack because he's giving me a terrible pain in my chest. I'm feeling a father energy. Yes, he's telling me he is your father. He wants you to know that was him singing to you as you walked by the river this morning. Do you understand this? (Yes, I nodded.) He says his brother Bill, who recently passed, and his sister who died as a baby both joined him in the singing. Do you understand this?*

(Again, I nodded yes.) He's telling me the three of them combined their energies to make the song strong enough to pierce the veil. He's so happy you heard the singing and felt the love.

My heart burst with such joy! Tears ran down my face as I sat listening to Roy and this miraculous message from my father. The details left no doubt it was really his spirit standing behind me. Roy had no way of knowing about my father's heart attack, my Uncle Bill's passing the year before, or their first-born sibling—a baby girl who died just a few days after her birth. Finally, the years of longing for connection with my father were over. I was absolutely speechless as a feeling of deep peace filled my heart. These old, familiar words filled my thoughts: *"This is the peace that passes all understanding."*

I had no time to wonder about the source of this inspiration because Roy continued giving me more information from the other side.

There's a woman showing herself to me. It feels like a mother energy. Is your mother on the other side? (No, I answered.) She says she is your "mother-of-the-heart." Do you know what that means? (No, I answered again.) She's showing me her flower garden. She loved to plant her flowers every spring.

This last clue left no doubt—this spirit had to be my dear Golda! I laughed out loud with the joy of recognizing her spirit. I had such delight about connecting with her again. Without thinking, I asked, "Was that really you in my living room two days after your funeral?" Roy spoke for my mother-in-law, saying, "Yes, of course that was me. You already know that. Why are you asking such a foolish question?" Again, I laughed out loud because this spirit sounded just like my dear Golda when she was with me here on earth. She was never one to mince words!

Roy continued with more messages from the other side until our thirty-minute session was finished. I left in a daze. This experience of spirit communication was as mind-blowing as Golda's first visitation. Walking across campus, this quote came wafting into my awareness: "Once the mind is expanded it can never go back to where it was." Indeed, I immediately understood that I couldn't go back to my old ways of thinking; my world would never be the same. That day I experienced a monumental shift in consciousness that included these new beliefs: *Spirit communication is real. Our deceased loved ones really can pierce the veil and send messages. They are around and watching us as we go about our lives. Their love is eternal. We are always connected.*

The experience of having my own reading was thrilling—so much more exciting than reading books about spirit communication. My heart yearned for more, and this led to another life-changing, risky decision. Roy lived in Montreal, Canada, yet I invited him to my home in Indiana to do readings for my friends and clients. In retrospect, this was another defining moment in my career, but at the time, I didn't think of it that way. Neither did I realize that as I kept following my passion for spirit communication, I was breaking new ground and creating a career path that was growing more and more different from the norm. Remember, this was 1990, before the TV shows like *Crossing Over, Ghost Whisperer,* and *The Medium.* Spirit communication was still very much in the closet and traditional grief therapists did not even consider discussing spiritual matters. I guess I didn't take time to think about that—I was simply following my heart.

For the next ten years, Roy and I worked together at my home. It was a match made in heaven—pardon the pun! He became my mentor and teacher for my own spiritual awakening as well as my evolution into a healer—a person who works with spiritual energy to help others heal emotionally and physically. For these weekends, my responsibilities were first, to educate people about the benefits of receiving messages from their deceased loved ones, and then to fill Roy's schedule with those who were open to the possibility. Contrary to what you might think, since we were doing this in rural Indiana in the early nineties, this was an easy job—I simply shared my joy about connecting with my dad and Golda; others wanted the same joy and the deeper healing of their grief. The people who came for readings were mostly my clients, who then allowed me to listen to the tape recordings of their session. Do the math: I listened to 252 tapes each year for ten years—that's approximately 2,500 readings. These years of working with Roy were like getting a doctorate in spiritual studies with a specialty in life after death and spirit communication.

During our work together, I became fascinated with communication from the spirits of miscarried babies and those who crossed over due to infant death. At first, it was a bit unbelievable, even to me. I found myself wondering, *"How could this be? A baby who never talked can send words to loved ones?"* Roy's explanation made sense to me, *"It's the soul of the baby who is sending the message. Souls have abilities beyond what we can ever know. You'll be amazed when you cross over."*

These spirit babies came again and again, announcing to parents, grand-parents, siblings, and other relatives, "I still exist. We are still connected. Our love is forever." Each time, I witnessed grieving loved ones heal at a much deeper level. As they related their experience of spiritual connection, we'd hug and I'd feel a little spark of joy in my heart. By this time I understood this little burst of energy was my soul saying, *"You are on the right path."*

On occasion, a spirit baby would come through Roy with a loving message and the client would say, "I have no idea who this is. You must be mistaken." Then, weeks later, after talking with an older relative, the client might tell me, "Oh, yes, a baby died in our family, but nobody ever talked about that. It was a secret." This was not an unusual scenario. So I learned that even babies we don't know or remember can stay connected. If you'll remember, a baby from my own family showed up in my first reading with Roy. I happened to know about this aunt who died thirty-some years before I was born; but she was never in my thoughts. And yet she came. The connection was still there. Amazing!

People did not come for readings asking or expecting to connect with the spirit of a deceased baby. They didn't even know this was possible. They came with an entirely different agenda, like connecting with a recently deceased loved one. Imagine their shock and surprise when a baby showed up with a message: "Don't be sad. I'm happy where I am." Sometimes people had been carrying a secret grief for forty or fifty years—especially if it was a miscarriage that had never been made public. Each time, the miracle of connection allowed their grief to vanish—*poof!* One woman said to me, "I always expected to see my baby again when I died. I know she will be waiting for me at the gates of heaven. It's so amazing that she came to me now while I'm still alive. What a blessing!" In the moment, my heart opened, and I heard my soul say once again *"You are on the right path."*

Part I
Spirit Babies Send Healing

Everyone enjoys a love story. Part I of *Connected for All Time: Book One* is filled with many beautiful love stories portraying soul love as a powerful force that reaches across time and space. These real-life stories show how signs and messages coming from spirit babies activate healing and ignite feelings of peace, joy, and love in the hearts of grieving family members. This section illustrates a well-known spiritual truth: *Love is the most powerful healing force in the universe.*

CHAPTER ONE

—∞—

Powerful Medicine
of the Spirit Babies

We Incas want the world to know
of the healing power of the spirit babies.
—Wachan, Inca Medicine Man

Meeting Wachan, an Inca medicine man, was one of those synchronistic events that could only have been arranged by Spirit. It was truly a God-Moment! Let me tell you how this chance encounter unfolded.

On a clear, sunny day in January, I set off with Mary, my friend and fellow healer. We left Phoenix and drove North on I-17 headed for Sedona, Arizona. Our intention was to spend some time in meditation on Bell Rock. This rather famous place is called an energy vortex because it is filled with high frequency energy that makes it easier for visitors to have mystical experiences. It is said that the veil between the earthly world and the spiritual world is very thin at Bell Rock. Just being in the energy of this special place forges a deeper connection to the sacred. Our journey to Sedona was planned with that specific purpose in mind.

We parked the car and began walking toward the majestic red rock formed in the shape of a bell. My attention was immediately drawn to an Indian man walking ten paces ahead of us with a very large drum attached to his back. This drum reached from the back of his head to the back of his knees—it was just amazing! He was dressed in traditional Indian attire, and a long black braid fell over the drum. Surprisingly, I felt a strong magnetic pull connecting me to this stranger though I had no earthly idea why. At first sight, I wanted to run over to him and start a conversation, but I hesitated because a woman companion walked beside him. The two of them disappeared down a path to the right that led to a cave-like area under Bell Rock. My assumption was they came to do some healing work and would not appreciate the company of strangers.

With great anticipation Mary and I hiked up to the lower levels of this majestic formation. We each found a little niche where we could sit comfortably leaning against the ancient red rocks. Within minutes the earth began to reverberate with the sound of the Indian drum. The hypnotic ancient rhythms were enhanced by the exquisite sounds of a flute.

The music was magical! I felt myself sink into the energy of this spiritual place, leave my everyday thoughts and concerns behind, and drift into the world of Spirit. I remember thinking, "The Universe is giving me the gift of my own private vision quest." My heart opened to the awesome knowing that Spirit was blessing me. Tears of joy and gratitude flowed down my face.

My focus went to the half-finished manuscript for this book about healing grief after the death of an infant. I was stuck in the writing process and wanted to start flowing again. From my heart, I asked Spirit for assistance. *Show me how to do this. How can I best help grieving loved ones understand their baby is now a spirit? How can I get my message out to the world?* Then I was given this vision—it was like daydreaming.

I saw my Spirit-self walking like the Pied Piper with hundreds of spirit babies following me as I moved from this world into the afterlife. There was no grief or sadness as we flowed easily along with a sense of great purpose. We all simply slipped through an opening in the clouds and disappeared from sight. These words came unbidden: *This is your soul mission. You are here to connect the spirit babies with their grieving loved ones. There is no death. There is only love. Take this message to the world.*

The vision faded and all was quiet for a few moments. My attention was captured once again by the melodious flute music as it danced with the rhythm of the drum. The vibration of the ancient music filled my every cell and carried me once again into the world of Spirit. The visions continued with more scenes that touched my heart so deeply I could hardly breathe. For a long time there was only light—no words. I have no idea how much time passed before I came back to an awareness of this earth.

The drumming ended just as Mary and I made our way down the side of Bell Rock and meandered towards our car. The Indian and his companion came strolling along the same path. Feeling a bit awkward, I ran up to him to thank him for providing an opening to the spirit world. As we talked, I felt compelled to tell him about the book and the visions that came to me. He smiled, put his hands together like he was praying, and bowed in honor of the visions. With great humility, this awesome being spoke to us in broken English.

My name is Wachan. I am an Inca medicine man. This is my wife who plays the flute. Our home is in Peru near the famous mountain called Machu Pichu (Ma-choo Pee-choo). We are living here in Sedona for now and teaching others about our ways. I must tell you about the spirit babies in the Inca traditions.

We believe spirit babies surround Pachatusan (Pa-cha-too-san), a sacred mountain in Peru not far from Machu Pichu. This sacred place is our burial ground for babies. Since time began all Incas make the trek to Pachatusan when death comes to a baby. It's an ancient Inca tradition.

The spirits of these babies form a big circle high in the sky all around the mountain. When you go there and listen quietly, you can hear their beautiful music. The sound is so pure it sounds like the angels are singing. Just the baby spirits live there; that's why the sound is so pure. We believe the spirits of the babies bring us our purity—they bring us light. And so we call them "the keepers of purity."

If you go to the mountain at sunset, you can hear the babies singing their beautiful music. I take many visitors there. I ask them to listen and tell me what they hear. They tell me, "It sounds like the wind is singing." Then I tell them of the babies who live there.

Pachatusan is also called "the medicine man mountain." All Inca healers (medicine men) go there for their spiritual training. When you come back from the mountain you are ready to work. That is the tradition.

The Inca people also go to this sacred place for healing if they are sick in mind, body, or spirit. The healing energy of the spirit babies at Pachatusan is powerful medicine. We Incas want the world to know of the healing power of the spirit babies.

So I give you these words as a gift for your book.

And I give you my blessings.

My friend and I went to Bell Rock seeking an experience of expanded consciousness and deeper connection to Spirit. It seems Spirit heard our prayers and blessed us with this synchronistic encounter. Meeting Wachan was like God saying to me, *"You must write this book. You must complete your soul mission."* I continue to marvel at the unseen mystical powers that brought this holy man into my path so I could tell the world about the

Inca traditions and the healing power of the spirit babies. It is often said, "Spirit works in strange and wondrous ways." Undoubtedly, it does!

In our modern American culture we have no traditions about spirit babies becoming healers for the family. However, you will see as you read these fascinating stories that we are no different from the ancient Inca people. Indeed, this book is filled with story after story showing that, even now, in twenty-first-century America, when a beloved baby goes to heaven, the spirit of that baby remains connected to family and other loved ones here on earth. The force that connects them is soul love—the powerful medicine that heals grief.

This book is about the healing power of the spirit babies.
They heal grief through connection.

CHAPTER TWO

Recognizing Signs and Messages

I suspect we are all recipients of cosmic love notes.
Messages, omens, voices, cries, revelations, and appeals
are homogenized into each day's events.
If only we knew how to listen, to read the signs.
—*Sam Keen, Author*

After the death of an infant, parents and other loved ones often yearn for connection to that beloved soul who came and stayed such a short time here on earth. It's common for them to pray, "Please send me some kind of sign. I need to know you are okay." You may have found yourself saying this same prayer. Did you receive an answer? If your response is yes, you've already experienced the healing power of connection. In *Reunions,* Dr. Raymond Moody reports that approximately seventy-five percent of parents who have lost an infant or young child report some kind of contact.

If your prayer went unanswered, you may be wondering why. The explanation is simple—you have not yet learned to understand the language of your spirit baby. While doing the interviews for this book, I found this to be the case time and time again. This new language is easy to learn once you develop the skill of recognizing the many different ways your beloved infant sends signs and messages across the chasm that separates heaven and earth.

The following collection of stories shows that, indeed, spirit babies exist and have the ability to send powerful medicine to their loved ones who are dealing with devastating grief after the loss of an infant. These powerful healers routinely send signs, messages, dreams, and other "cosmic love notes" that are meant to uplift grieving loved ones and fill their hearts with peace, love, and joy. These healing stories come from ordinary people who have learned to listen with their hearts and read the signs.

It's been my experience that these accounts of spirit babies abound if you are open to hearing them. Once I set my intention to write this book, stories of communication from spirit babies flowed to me from virtually everywhere:

individual healing sessions, workshop participants, networking contacts, perfect strangers, and many other divinely guided connections. My friends laughingly call me the "story magnet" because stories about spirit babies are continuously finding me even as this book goes to press.

Doing the interviews for this book was such a joy! I listened to people's stories, affirmed their experience, cried with them, laughed with them, and shared sacred space with all the mothers, fathers, and grandparents who were willing to take me into their hearts.

Several contributors reported that they had never told their experience to anyone else because they were afraid others might think:

> *"You're just crazy and having delusions."*
>
> *"You're making it up out of wishful thinking."*
>
> *"You're desperate and looking for any relief."*
>
> *"You're not accepting the finality of your infant's death."*

Others had told their experience of spirit baby communication and felt criticized instead of supported. Thereafter, they stopped sharing and kept their precious healing stories to themselves. One young mother said in a whisper, "My experience of spirit communication from my baby is much too sacred to risk sharing it with just anybody. I couldn't bear to hear any negative comments about the signs and messages I receive from my spirit baby. You are safe because you believe." Repeatedly, mothers, fathers, grandparents, and siblings told me, "I've never shared this story before." Consequently, the healing power of the spirit babies is one of the best-kept secrets of our modern-day society.

Storytelling is one of the ancient ways of teaching in cultures of old. To this day it's still one of the best ways to impart wisdom and healing. In the words of Clarissa Pinkola Estes, author of *Women Who Run with the Wolves*, "Stories do not 'cure' problems, they offer new choices, new understandings, renewed hope. These are the elements that treat the soul." With this in mind, I invite you to read the sacred stories in this book with an open mind and an open heart. They will help you learn to recognize the twelve different ways your beloved infant can send signs and messages.

It is my deepest hope that, as you read, you will open to the soul love flowing from your own spirit baby and all the spirit babies in this book. As the Inca tradition teaches, they are the keepers of purity and light who come to bring the gift of healing to your aching heart.

1. Feeling a Presence

After the loss of an infant many loved ones report feeling a presence, even though they cannot perceive anything with their other senses. This presence is not to be discounted just because it's subtle. It's a valid way for spirit babies to send love into the hearts of their family members here on earth.

Into My Space

Tammy's heart was filled with devastating grief when her son was stillborn. Some relief came a few months later when she was able to feel a connection with the spirit of this baby she named Charles.

My infant son is in heaven but I feel him around me quite often. He comes to me as a presence—like I feel somebody has come into my space. I don't see or hear anything, but I get this special feeling in my heart and a knowing that he's near. It's amazing that something so subtle can bring so much peace to my grieving heart! In the beginning months of my grief, I kept myself extra busy to block the pain. Now that I've slowed down, I can feel my son's presence in the quiet times. Perhaps he was always around but I was too busy to notice.

A Connection of Love

Heidi has no doubt about her eternal connection with Brittany Rose, the spirit of her baby girl who died in the womb just weeks before her delivery date.

In the beginning I felt Brittany Rose's presence as a connection of love. It was more like I felt my love for her and her love for me. It's the love that goes on; a mother's love is forever. We are so connected because I nurtured her, I grew her, I nourished her for eight months in my womb. I took care of her and felt her kick, so I know she is a child of this family and always will be.

The loving feelings I have for her now are triggered by thoughts of her, when I see her picture, or see something that reminds me of her, such as one of the many angels I have in our home. I have good-feeling memories, like when I look through her baby album, or I spot the bunny that hangs around the house. I don't think Brittany is in the bunny, or influences the bunny to hop through our yard. I believe God may send the bunny because He knows that bunnies remind me of my sweet angel, Brittany.

Feeling a presence is a valid way of sensing the spirit of your precious infant who is now on the other side. Trust it. Believe it when you get that feeling. Acknowledge it by sending a mental message back, "Thanks for coming to visit me today. I'm glad you are around. I love you and I know you love me." You can send mental messages or speak out loud. Your spirit baby can hear you either way.

2. Getting Angel Bumps

Spirit babies have the ability to send energy and cause goose bumps on your arms or a little shiver through your entire body. It's just another way of letting you know they are around. Some people call these physical sensations confirmation chills or angel bumps.

Confirmation for Mimi

Sarah, a holistic nutritionist, has a strong belief in life after death. She shared this sweet story about spirit communication from her beloved grandson.

> *I started hearing a little voice whispering to me a few days after Christopher, my first grandson, went to live in heaven. Sometimes I can't make out any words but the whispering sound is there. Other times I actually hear "Mimi." That's the special name our family uses for "Grandma." Each time the whispering comes, I get these goose bumps on my arms; my friend calls them angel bumps. These little angel bumps help me trust my senses and believe Christopher is calling me.*

3. Playing With Electrical Devices

Because spirit babies are energy beings it's possible for them to manipulate energy here on earth. Playing with electricity seems to be an easy way for them to make their presence known to their loved ones in the physical world. They often make lights, TVs and radios flash on and off. It's their way of signaling a hello.

Flashing Christmas Lights

Jill treasures this spirit communication from her angel baby Karen, who transitioned seven days after birth because of a malformed heart.

> *It was Christmas and I wanted to honor our daughter's spirit as part of the family, so I put a beautifully framed picture of our baby Karen by the Christmas tree. During the holiday season I often sat*

alone by the tree, staring at the beautiful lights, and thinking about our baby in heaven. Then one night the tree lights started blinking off and on. I checked all the electrical connections, and everything seemed fine. Yet, when I sat down again, the lights blinked once more. Then it dawned on me—the spirit of our baby was sending me a message, "I'm here. I love you!" I wept with pure joy at this Christmas miracle of connection. It's the best gift I ever received.

Sing a Song for Me

Heather calls herself "Mom to three angels" because she has three spirit babies in heaven—Melissa, Conner and Lane. She is highly intuitive and receives signs, messages, and dreams quite regularly from all three of her children on the other side.

One of the songs I picked for Lane's funeral was "Sailing" by Rod Stewart. The words are so touching, and I wanted it played at his funeral. Sadly, when they tried to play this song at the service, the CD player malfunctioned. The words "no data" kept showing up— I've never seen that happen before or since with that CD player.

A few weeks later, my husband insisted we take a little trip to just get away. It was my birthday, and I was sitting in our motel room when I started hearing Rod Stewart singing "Sailing." It was on rather low, so I walked out the door, and looked around the parking lot, but no one was out there. Finally, I discovered it was coming from inside our car. The CD player that said "no data" at the funeral was in the back seat of our car. Magically, it was now working and playing this special song for me!

At the end of the song the music just stopped, as if someone turned off the CD player. I knew this was Lane's way of saying, "Happy Birthday, Mama!" I've often wondered just exactly how he got that CD player to come on and play just one song. It's a mystery and a miracle!

4. Sending a Song

Did you ever find yourself humming a tune without realizing what song is playing through your mind? There is usually a significant message when you figure out the words or the title. Have you ever turned on the radio and heard a song that reminds you of your baby who lives on the other side? Spirit babies have the ability to send a song into your head or influence you to turn on the radio at exactly the right time to hear a special song that will remind you of their love and connection or express a specific message.

A Song in My Head

Helen lost a little girl named Rebecca just weeks before her due date. A few months later Helen noticed a song playing in her head; it was "Somewhere Over the Rainbow." She was thinking of Rebecca as all the words came effortlessly into her mind, although it had been years since she had even heard the song. In that moment she knew it was a song sent from heaven.

A Song on the Radio

After Dana's miscarriage, she began hearing the song "I Hope You Dance" come on the radio when she was at a low point. Dana was convinced her baby was telling her to enjoy life. She said, "He doesn't want me to be miserable. It does pick up my spirits; I usually laugh out loud when I hear this reminder song!"

Out of Africa

Emily spent her short life of seven months in the hospital before making her transition. Diane, her mother, shared this story about her spirit daughter sending a song.

> *Our Emily seemed to really like music. My husband would record music for her and bring it to the hospital. Her favorite song was "Out of Africa." She loved that tape! We put speakers in the neonatal bassinet near each side of her head. When the medical staff wanted her to relax, they would play that particular song. Then she would really mellow out, and her oxygen levels would go way up.*

> *We felt inspired to play "Out of Africa" at her funeral Mass, and it really touched everyone. People told me there was not a dry eye in the church while Emily's song was playing. After the funeral, we gave all the tapes and the music system to the neonatal unit.*

> *I have a friend, Annette, who believes our deceased loved ones can provide guidance and assistance in our daily lives. She often prays to Emily's spirit when she has a need. One day, Annette was so sick driving home that she didn't think she was going to make it to her house. She called upon Emily's spirit, saying, "Oh, Emily, you're going to have to help me." She pulled off the road to rest and turned on her radio. Of all things, Emily's favorite song, "Out of*

Africa" was playing at that very moment! Annette was completely overcome with awe and gratitude. As soon as she got home, she called to tell me. This was such a blessed healing from Emily.

I Believe

Heather was driving home from the hospital just hours after Lane died in the Neonatal Intensive Care Unit (NICU, pronounced "nick-you"). She heard a song that spoke to her heart, and immediately knew her baby was sending her a message that he was okay. It was the country song by Diamond Rio called "I Believe." Some of the words to this song are included here so you can understand the significance of this message.

I believe; oh, I believe

That when you die your life goes on:

It doesn't end here when you're gone.

Every soul is filled with light,

It never ends and if I'm right,

Our love can even reach across eternity.

Heather said these lyrics played at a moment when she desperately needed to hear them. Because her heart opened wide as she was listening to this healing song, she believes that God and her baby were bringing her a message of comfort.

5. Sending a Sign

Spirits often correspond by sending a sign to their loved ones. It could be a coin, a feather, a yellow rose, or some other symbol that keeps appearing and lights up your heart. You might even notice that something has been moved in the house; spirit babies have the ability to manipulate physical things to get your attention. These signs are subtle and are often missed. If your heart lights up as you see a symbol, trust that it is coming from your baby. Acknowledge it with gratitude and ask your baby to continue sending this same sign. It will be your private signal—the way your spirit baby says "I love you."

Pennies Up High

Jeannie was in deep grief after losing her grandson William. She didn't really believe in spirit communication until she had her own experience.

I was filled with despair after William's death. I thought my heart would break with grief for my daughter, her husband and our whole family. I spent a lot of time talking to William's spirit, but I never dreamed he could send me a sign. Then one day while cleaning the family room, I discovered two pennies high on top of the entertainment center. As I picked them up I was filled with curiosity. Who could have placed them there? It was so high they couldn't have just fallen out of someone's pocket.

I asked my husband, the cleaning lady, my adult children, and any friends who had been in the house over the past months. Nobody knew anything about these pennies—they all just shook their heads and looked mystified. Finally, it dawned on me that William put them there hoping I would find them and recognize it as a little hello from him. I was thrilled when this idea came to me. I know it's true because I got chill bumps everywhere as the thought came into my head.

Let's Play, Mom!

Connie lost her first child, an infant daughter she named Holly. She was still in deep grief when she began to notice something very intriguing. Connie had a little angel pin bought in honor of her daughter's memory, and no matter where she left her angel pin it rarely stayed in the same place. At first, Connie thought her mind was playing tricks on her because she was too stressed. However, one night Connie deliberately placed the pin in her jewelry box, and yet she found it on the kitchen counter the next morning. Finally, it dawned on her that Holly's spirit was being mischievous! Evidently, Holly loves to play hide and seek! Now Connie laughs each time the angel turns up in another strange place. Her heart sings at this opportunity to play with her baby. It has been very healing for Connie to participate in this little game.

The Insistent Dime

After Josh died, Beth joined an infant loss support group where she met Heidi, who was healing from the loss of her beloved baby girl named Brittany Rose. The two women quickly bonded and spent time together outside the group. While traveling with Heidi, Beth experienced their two spirit babies playing a little game with them.

Heidi and I became fast friends after meeting each other in our infant loss support group. She was always finding coin messages from her spirit baby, and I was grumbling because I had never found a coin from Josh. We were sharing a hotel room on a trip to Las Vegas, and Heidi found a dime. As she put the dime on the dresser, she said a quick "Thanks for the sign, Brittany Rose!"

Later she found a dime on the bed and went to put it on the dresser with the other one. But there was no dime on the dresser. It was gone! She asked me if I had moved it, but I had no idea what she was talking about. That evening Heidi found another dime, this time on the bathroom floor, and again the dime on the dresser was missing! We began to suspect that Brittany Rose was moving the dime to play hide-and-seek. Then Heidi found the dime alongside the nightstand! This dime showed up four or five times until Heidi said, "Beth, I think this dime must be for you, not me! I think it's from Josh!" I was happy to have the coin, but I still wasn't one hundred percent sure it was from Josh. Strangely, the dime never moved again! Maybe that's because we finally understood it was from Josh, not Brittany Rose.

I got home from the trip and cleaned out my purse—which means I dumped it upside down and shook everything out. I sorted out all the stuff, moved my change to our coin bank, and put everything back in my purse very carefully. I'm sure there was no loose change left in there. I was leaving the house so I threw my purse over my shoulder and headed out the door. Just then I spotted a scrap of paper on the floor and bent to pick it up. Out of my purse flew a dime! I picked it up saying, "Excellent! Thanks, Josh!"

6. Playing the Numbers Game

Sometimes a spirit baby on the other side will give you a nudge to look at the clock (or a sign or a license plate) to see a specific pattern of numbers. It might be double numbers, triple numbers, or a significant sequence, such as a birth date. In these moments your heart will light up with the joy of spirit communication. You may also get angel bumps to signal you to pay attention to this message.

Honoring August 10th

Charlotte had a great deal of grief after miscarrying a baby girl she named Brenda Sue. She spent a lot of time crying and releasing. Eventually, she was able to clear most of her heartache, grief, shame, and guilt. The miscarriage was August 10 (8th month, 10th day), so each year on that date she does a sacred ceremony honoring the spirit of her baby.

After a few years Charlotte noticed that she became aware of her digital clock at 8:10 in the morning and 8:10 in the evening. No matter what she was doing she would look up and see 8:10—a delightful but meaningless surprise. This went on for weeks before she finally understood it was a little love-tap from Brenda Sue. Now each time she notices 8:10, she smiles and gets a little glow in her heart knowing the spirit of her baby is drawing her attention to the clock.

As she finished telling her story, Charlotte announced, "I believe my baby wants me to honor the day she went to heaven. Playing this little number game is our way of staying connected."

7. Receiving Ideas and Inspiration

Did you ever wonder where creative ideas and inspirations come from? I believe they come from the spirit world—sent by our individual souls, our spirit guides, ever-loving angels, and our loved ones on the other side. They send us guidance because they want to help us along our earthly journey. The stories in this section show us that spirit babies also have the ability to send ideas and inspiration.

Your loved ones in Spirit often send inspiration and guidance to help you find ways to alleviate your grief. They want you to heal your terrible heartache and live in joy once again. Many times your spirit baby is actually with you, sending thoughts and inspirations that seem to come out of the blue. You may receive inspirations like: "Buy that book," "Go this way," or "Go see that movie."

One grieving mother had just such an experience when she was driving for the first time to a support meeting. Tammy was lost and couldn't find the street mentioned in her directions. As she wandered around, she suddenly got the idea she should turn "right here, right now!" Tammy followed her inner prompting and, within a few blocks, was back on track. Tammy tells everyone that Ashley, her baby in heaven, was guiding her to a place where she would find relief for her deep grief.

These kinds of inspired messages from the spirit realm offer love, support, and guidance as you continue to live and learn here in the physical world.

This Book Is for Me!

Candice's grief was still all-consuming six months after Sudden Infant Death Syndrome (SIDS) claimed her son John. Nothing seemed to ease her terrible heartache. Hoping for a distraction, she went to the local bookstore to find the exciting novel her friend had recommended. Unable to locate it, she wandered aimlessly around until she felt an urge to go down a certain aisle. There, Candice found herself looking at *Healing Grief, Reclaiming Life After Any Loss* by James Van Praagh. This book opened a whole new world to her because Van Praagh, a spiritual medium, presents proof of survival messages from loved ones on the other side. This was the first time Candice entertained the idea of her baby continuing to exist in the spirit world. In retrospect, she is sure her baby's spirit led her to this book.

8. Sending a Message Through Human Beings

Have you ever noticed that someone will say the words you need to hear, sing a song, or tell a joke, and *poof*, your loved one is in your heart and on your mind? People bring these important messages at synchronistic times because your loved one in Spirit is inspiring the words and thoughts in order to give you a message born of great love.

Froggy Gifts!

Fran has a deep love connection with the spirit of her grandson Harrison. This powerful spirit baby even inspires Fran's friends to deliver cosmic love notes from heaven.

It's been seven years, and people still give me frogs out the blue without knowing why. A new friend was recently on a vacation and felt compelled to buy me a frog. She gave it to me saying, "I don't know what's going on here, but I got this persistent message to buy this frog for you." I'm so happy that she followed her intuition because I know the frog came from my grandson Harrison.

I get messages from the spirit of Harrison all the time. His skin was green when he was first born, so I lovingly called him "my little frog." Right after his transition, I saw frogs everywhere— they showed up as stuffed toys and figurines, as well as images on license plates, greeting cards, and magazines. At first, I didn't pay much attention, but then I finally realized these were little signs from my grandson. It is uplifting to know he is still with me and inspires me to notice all these froggy messages!

A lot of people would discount these signs. However, I believe it's him because I never noticed frogs before Harrison, and now I do. A warm glow creeps into my heart whenever Harrison comes to mind, and I feel such joy in the moment—just like he was here!

These frog gifts always come when I'm feeling down, challenged by life, or need some reassurance. I know it's Harrison telling me that he cares and is watching over me. We were so bonded during his short four months of life, and it is reassuring to know our heart bond is as strong as ever! It is fascinating that he can inspire other people to buy me frogs! Each time I feel so loved—and I am!

9. Sending a Message Through Animals

We already know many human beings have the ability to use telepathic communication with animals. Spirits, including your spirit baby, can also use the same process to send a message of love through animals. We do not know exactly how they do this, but stories about this phenomenon abound and show us that it is, indeed, quite common.

Two Male Cardinals

Just months after Darlene lost twin boys, she began to notice that two male cardinals would frequent the tree near her balcony. It seemed whenever she relaxed outside, she would spot the two bright red birds sitting side by side. Each time she saw them, a rush of warm feelings blossomed immediately in her chest, and she felt excited as she thought of her boys. Darlene's twins did not become the birds, but rather influenced them to sit side by side, an unusual behavior for territorial males!

A Bunny Brings Love

Cheryl is a devoted mother and grandmother, and was totally devastated after the loss of her grandson. She once sat with a psychic who said, "Your grandson is going to send you a message through a bunny." Cheryl thought this was ridiculous and actually scoffed at the idea. The next weekend she walked down her front sidewalk to pick up the Sunday paper and was quite surprised to see a small rabbit nibbling on clover in her front yard. The bunny just sat and watched her come closer and closer—he didn't even try to hop away. Cheryl suddenly remembered the psychic's prediction. She burst out laughing and looked up to the heavens saying, "Well, hello, Will!" Interestingly enough, the bunny stayed around for almost two weeks. Each time Cheryl or her husband went outside, the bunny just sat very still and stared at them.

Five Deer at the Gravesite

One day Tracey opened her heart to God and prayed for a sign from Peter, her spirit son. She was both surprised and delighted when her prayer was answered.

On one of Peter's birthdays, I was at his gravesite feeling really sad—you know, missing him terribly. I was by myself and I prayed, "Just give me a sign that you know I'm here." Within seconds, five deer came running by. It was really bizarre! You can usually see the deer at dusk, but this happened in the middle of the day!

Later, I looked up the symbolism of deer crossing your path in Ted Andrew's book, Animal Speak. *He states, "When deer show up there is an opportunity to express gentle love that will open new doors to adventure for you." How true! It truly is an adventure to explore these experiences of spirit communication from Peter.*

A Spiritual Butterfly

Kalilia was devastated when she miscarried her first baby late in the pregnancy. To honor this baby girl, she named her Miracle. Kalilia received this sweet gift of healing from her spirit daughter.

I began receiving signs from Miracle within days of her transition to heaven. First, a really big, beautiful monarch butterfly came and sat on a floral arrangement during the memorial service. My eye was drawn right to it. Then, I was staring out the window driving home and every time we stopped the same beautiful monarch was fluttering by my window. I thought it was very strange at the time. How could a butterfly keep up with a car? When we arrived home, the same butterfly was sitting on the pink azaleas by the front door. I knew something spiritual was going on with this butterfly. I felt like it was Miracle waiting to see that I got home and saying, "I'm with you still."

10. Sending a Message Through Blooming Plants

Sometimes spirits share comfort and little hellos by sending a blooming message. Pay attention to the bloom that comes on a significant date or at an unusual time of year—it just may be your loved one saying, "I'm still with you and I love you!"

A Trumpeting Hello

Heather spoke with awe and wonder in her voice as she shared this story of continued connection with her beloved spirit baby named Conner.

I have this trumpeting angel plant that I just love. It's usually an outdoor plant, but I keep mine in the house. It's a little green vine that produces a long, pure white flower that looks like a trumpet; hence, the name trumpeting angel. The flower is extremely delicate and actually dies the same day it appears. These plants only bloom once a year, and they stay on the same cycle every year; mine usually blooms in the winter, right after Christmas.

A little miracle happened with this plant two years after Conner's passing. His birthday is October 6. On that day I walked into the room where I keep the trumpeting angel plant, and there was a delicate white flower in full bloom. The little bud just popped right open on Conner's birthday! It bloomed three months ahead of schedule, so I knew it was a spiritual message. I took it as a sign from Conner saying, "Mama, I know you know it's my birthday, and it's okay to remember."

A Pink Rose in November

Heidi was terrified that her second baby might die because she was born two months early. Then a miracle brought peace to this mother's heart.

Brittany was still within my womb, but she had no heartbeat; I had yet to deliver her lifeless body. Friends from work sent me a huge arrangement of pink roses to honor our loss. I remember it like it was yesterday. I was sitting on my living room couch staring at those gorgeous flowers when the name "Rose" came to me. It immediately became her middle name! Since then, roses, especially pink, have a special meaning for me. Brittany is my little rosebud in heaven.

After losing Brittany Rose, I had another baby girl, who was delivered two months early. We decided to name her Jessica Rose. She was in the hospital for the whole month of November and we didn't know day to day if she would make it. It was a very scary time.

We had a rose bush by our front door, but it had been dormant for at least two months. I came home from the NICU one day and saw this huge, beautiful pink rose on our bush. Roses don't bloom in Chicago in November! I took this as a sign from God that our new baby was going to be just fine. From that moment on, I was at peace about Jessica. I have a picture of this November rose in Jessica's photo album to remind me of God's beautiful pink-rose message.

11. Receiving a Message Using Various Senses

Spirit babies can communicate with loved ones through any of our various senses—sight, touch, smell, hearing and even taste. These messages are usually very subtle. In fact, they are so subtle that people may notice something very slight or fleeting and then doubt their own experience.

For instance, you might see flashes of light or catch a movement out of the corner of your eye. Then you turn to look and find nothing. Trust you are getting a glimpse into the spirit world. You really did see something with your spiritual eyes, but then you could not see it again with your physical eyes. This same experience can happen with any of your senses.

The following stories illustrate spirit babies communicating with loved ones by sending a little glimmer, a special smell, or a sound.

Little Glimmers

Over time Tracey learned to use her spiritual eyes to perceive the fleeting visits from her spirit baby named Peter. She treasures these mystical encounters.

I sometimes see movement out of the corner of my right eye—it's always the right side. I know without a doubt it's Peter, and I get so much peace from this. It usually happens when I'm really quiet and by myself. Often when I'm digging in the garden I'll see this "thing" out of the corner of my eye—it's not an object—it's a little something. It's weird, more like a sensation of seeing rather than really seeing something. The first few times it happened, I would look up but I would never see anything. Now, I don't bother to look; I just say, "Hi, Peter."

Gardening is my therapy. When I'm in my garden, I'm doing what I love, and I absolutely get lost in it. It's a time when I'm quiet, and I can open up my mind. It's my way of getting in touch with myself— perhaps you could say I'm in touch with my soul while I'm gardening. Peter takes advantage of these times to contact me. Of course, I'm always thrilled when I notice the little glimmer of his spirit energy! If I try to make it happen, it never works; so I just have to do my thing in the garden, and welcome his unexpected little hellos!

Pay Attention to Me!

Lane sends his mother, Heather, little reminders that they are still connected even though he is now a spirit baby in heaven.

It's been two years, and I still get really stressed out and feel myself missing Lane so intensely. At these times I let myself sink into the grief and just cry my heart out. A few days later I will get this smell that tells me Lane is all around me. The NICU has its own unique smell—a mixture of medicines, the babies, and the oil we used to massage the infants. This NICU smell is always the same, and whenever it flows in, I know Lane is contacting me to bring comfort to my aching heart.

I started experiencing this smell about eight months after his death, and it comes at least twice a month here lately. It happens anytime and anyplace—at the post office, the grocery store, a friend's house, and even in the car.

Sometimes I wonder, "Where has he gone? Is he not going to contact me?" Within days the smell will come. Then I feel like he's saying, "Mama, you shouldn't have to ask. I'm never far away."

Lane's always close, and whenever he sends me a message, I feel this overwhelming peace. I get such a warm feeling all through me and around me. I would love to have an aura picture taken, because I know he would somehow show up in my aura. He has passed from bodily form, but he has not gone far.

You have to be open-minded to receive messages. I can't believe that life ends at the grave—because it doesn't! Lane is around me all the time, but my life gets hectic, and then I don't get any messages. Like everyone else, I get caught up in life—suddenly the smell comes. Then I know he's saying, "Hey! Pay attention to me!"

Knock, Knock

While grieving the loss of premature twin boys, Darlene connected with a song entitled, "One Sweet Day." The lyrics include this message, "They are shining down from heaven, and you'll see them again one day." She called it our song, and it always touched her heart to hear it. About a year after losing the twins, Darlene was alone in her apartment one afternoon when "One Sweet Day" came on the radio. She turned up the volume until it was blaring. Then these fascinating events unfolded.

I heard five very loud knocks on the door. They had to be loud, because I could hear them over the blasting radio. I answered the door thinking it was a neighbor coming to complain about the loud music. Nobody was at the door or in sight up and down the hall. I went back in my apartment so I wouldn't miss this song that always uplifts me. Again, I heard five knocks on the door. When I opened the door and saw the empty hallway, I thought it was neighbor kids playing tricks. However, there was nowhere for them to hide, and they didn't have time to run away before I opened the door.

I continued listening to the blasting music, and the five knocks came a third time. This time a feeling came over me as I opened the door and walked out into the hallway. Suddenly, I realized it wasn't the neighbor kids—it was my spirit babies knocking to get my attention. I was so overcome that I fell to the floor sobbing—I couldn't move for a very long time. I lay there paralyzed, thanking them over and over for coming.

This experience was such a joyous healing! Every second of it is written on my heart forever. Looking back, I see that I actually invited this to happen. I'd been hearing spirit communication stories from other women in our infant grief support group. I kept sending this message to my boys, "I know you are close. I want to hear from you. Come and visit me." They certainly gave me what I asked for! I have no doubt they are alive in heaven, and I will see them again one day.

12. Synchronistic Experiences

Coincidences do not just occur. They are actually little messages or signs guided by Spirit, that is, by the many possible sources that engineer synchronicities: God, your own soul, your guardian angels, your spirit guides, your deceased loved ones, and your spirit baby as well.

Pay attention to everything that happens around you, and you will begin to see the synchronistic moments created by Spirit. Can you remember a time in your life when everything was flowing? You were in the right place at the right time, the right people showed up, needed information came to you out of the blue, or everything fell into place, with positive results and no effort on your part. That was a synchronistic experience.

Spirit often works behind the scenes in a subtle way to co-create events that are designed to give you an "Aha!" experience. You receive the benefit of these moments even when you are unaware of the source. However, it is much more fun when you get it—that Spirit is at work on your behalf. It brings a lot of comfort when your spirit baby blesses you with a synchronistic message, and confidence comes from feeling the divine guidance you experience as you move through life.

Pulling Strings From Heaven

Heather laughed with much joy as she told this fascinating story of a synchronistic meeting that brought healing to her grieving heart.

My husband and I went into Cracker Barrel for breakfast several months after Conner's death. We were standing in line waiting for a table, when my attention was drawn to a little baby right in front of us. His mother was holding him over her shoulder, and he kept reaching for me as he was cooing and smiling. He seemed so excited to see me! I was just as fascinated—I couldn't take my eyes off him. It was the strangest thing.

The proud mama volunteered, "My baby's name is Conner. It's so cute how he's reaching for you and it's so unusual, because he's very shy."

Of course, I was thinking that my baby would be about this age now and soon found myself telling this stranger about losing Conner. We discovered both our babies were born in October. Then this mother said the sweetest thing to me, "Maybe this is your baby's way of letting you know he's okay." That really touched my heart! Actually, I've come to believe this truly was a message from my Conner in heaven. What are the odds of this happening? I can only imagine how Conner and my angels in heaven were pulling strings behind the scenes!

Share Your Stories

All of these parents and grandparents were excited to share their stories for this book. I hope these will give you the validation you might need to trust that your subtle experiences of spirit communication are also real. Then you can believe that your spirit baby is sending you signs and messages that are intended to uplift your spirit and soothe your aching heart.

As you read the stories in this chapter, you may have found yourself thinking, "Oh, that happened to me. I didn't know that could be interpreted as a sign from our baby." I've heard this response again and again from grieving loved ones during interviews for this book, as well as from individual healing sessions and grief workshops. At first people tell me, "I don't think our baby has sent any signs." Later, after learning about the twelve different types of spirit communication they say, "I get it now! How sad. I had no clue, and I've been missing the messages."

Sharing stories is always very healing. I encourage you to talk to others about the little signs and messages from your beloved baby who is now a spirit. Remember, there are others out there who are silently hoping to find another person who can "talk stories."

♥   ♥   ♥

Summary of Chapter Two

1) The healing power of the spirit babies is one of the best-kept secrets of our modern-day society.

2) Spirit babies exist and have the ability to send powerful medicine to their loved ones who are dealing with devastating grief after the loss of an infant.

3) Your baby's spirit is constantly sending out signs, inspiring thoughts, sounds, and various other forms of communication. You may or may not be receiving them.

4) Learning to use your spiritual senses is the key to recognizing signs and messages from your spirit baby.

5) Shivers, chills up and down your spine, goose bumps or angel bumps everywhere are indications that your soul is recognizing the presence of spirit energy and wants you to pay attention.

6) Spirit babies can send signs and messages through all your senses— touch, smell, hearing, vision, taste, and feeling a presence.

7) Do not dismiss simply feeling a presence; it is a valid way of perceiving the spirit of your baby on the other side.

8) Spirit babies can also send ideas and inspiration to loved ones on earth.

9) Synchronistic meetings and events are created or guided by Spirit. Your spirit baby often engineers these. This being loves you dearly and inspires you to be in the right place at the right time so you can receive a blessing.

10) Spirit babies can send a message though animals, blooming plants, or ordinary human beings who say or do just the right thing for your healing.

CHAPTER THREE

———∿———

Angelic Assistance

The angels are powerful healers,
and you can work with them
to speed up their healing efforts.
There are no limits to angels' healing power.
—Doreen Virtue, Ph.D., Angel Therapist and Author

Angels are God's messengers of love. They exist in the energy of divine love, and they bring that healing energy of hope and peace to all human beings here on earth. They remind us that our purpose here is to give unconditional love and to receive it, and they help us learn how to do that. This is extremely important when you are healing from the loss of an infant. Opening your heart to the vibration of angelic love will heal your pain and uplift you so that you and your spirit baby can give and receive one another's love.

Gentle Signs of Ever-Loving Presence

Even though you may be completely unaware of it, angels are always with you. They make their presence known in very subtle ways, so it is easier to perceive them when you open all your soul senses. Angels can appear in different forms to different people. They may appear as angelic beings in long, flowing white robes, as little cherubs with wings, or as glowing lights with no form at all. You may feel the presence of angels or simply begin to know that they are around.

Angels usually work behind the scenes, so you might receive the results of their efforts without ever perceiving their presence. They may create synchronistic experiences, so you get what you need for healing. Or they may inspire you to find the right book or the right grief workshop that will assist you in moving a few steps forward on your journey. They may also connect you to earthly angels—ordinary people who are divinely guided to assist other human beings. These earthly angels usually have helpful information to share with you.

27

Regardless of how angels appear—or don't appear—trust that they are with you at all times. They only need your attention to make themselves known and will cheerfully give you gentle signs of their ever-loving presence.

Josh and Beth: The Scent of Angels

The death of a baby often causes bereaved loved ones to begin a spiritual journey in search of relief from their devastating grief. Beth began such a quest after losing her son Josh.

> *I was so depressed after Josh died. I was doing our support group at the hospital, weekly psychotherapy, and antidepressants, but nothing seemed to help. My therapist said, "I think you need to get in touch with the spiritual part of Josh."*
>
> *Soon after, I was lying in bed reading an angel book given to me by a friend. All of a sudden I smelled this "puff" of rose scent. It was like someone sprayed one of those atomizers. I thought it was so strange. I started sniffing everything to find the source of this scent. I was wearing a friend's T-shirt, so I thought it might be her perfume—but I had washed it already. I smelled the pillow. I smelled everything but couldn't find the source. I thought, "I'm crazy anyway." I went back to reading the book, and the very next line was, "You may even smell the scent of an angel—rose or jasmine."*
>
> *At first, I felt only confusion because there was no logical explanation. After reading that line, I said, "Okay, I get it!" It was an instantaneous shift for me. I realized that there's another level of being that we don't understand. I opened my mind to the possibility of spirits communicating with us, and ever since that moment, I see signs, and I believe! My depression was not totally gone, but this angel experience did bring me peace.*

Starlet and Sylvia: Feathers From Heaven

Sylvia met with me about a year after her infant daughter died of heart complications. Her face was radiant as she shared this angel story about Starlet.

> *Just weeks after Starlet's transition, my good friend and neighbor, Lorrie, was watching TV one morning with her son, Christian, who was four years old. Star never came home from the hospital, so they had only seen pictures of her. Suddenly Christian looked up and pointed up to the ceiling fan with a look of amazement on his*

face. Just then a tiny, beautiful, pure white feather came floating down and landed right in the palm of his hand.

Christian announced with big eyes, "Mama, Mama, Star gave me this feather. I saw Star! She looks like an angel in a long white dress. You know how the kitty used to shake herself and lose her fur? Angels do the exact same thing. Star wiggled her little shoulders like our kitty, and this feather came out for me."

For the next six or eight months, I received many pure white feathers. There was no logical explanation about where they came from—there were no birds around. I knew they were little love gifts from Star. I saved a few and put them in Star's memory book.

Your Baby Is an Angel Too

Your baby may show herself or himself to you as an angel. Indeed, many mothers, fathers, and other loved ones have reported having such visions. So, if you have seen your beloved baby looking like an angel, trust that you did not "just make it up," and you are not going crazy.

The Twins and Elizabeth: Cherubs Playing in Heaven

Six months after miscarrying twins, the parents, Elizabeth and Richard, attended a special outdoor ceremony that the hospital holds annually in recognition of prenatal loss. During the service, Elizabeth received a vision that is written on her heart forever.

Just as the pastor was beginning her speech, many of the grieving family members started to weep. At that moment, a feeling of great sadness flowed through my entire body, and I was guided to look towards the sky.

My vision opened to an incredible scene amidst the soft billowy clouds. There was a heavenly playground, with dozens of cupids playing on swings and bikes. After a moment I saw that two of the cupids were our twins, laughing and swinging and having a wonderful time. The playground was filled with clouds so that when children fall, they have a soft landing. All the spirit babies looked so adorable with their little cupid wings. Such a wonderful glimpse of heaven! As I watched our twins sharing a bike, I heard an angelic voice say, "But wait! We're all happy here! There's no reason for you to be sad."

The scene came and went in a flash, but it had a profound healing effect on my grief. Relief flowed over me, and once again my heart filled with peace, knowing our twins are safe, happy and well cared for by God and the other angels.

Angels Take Care of Spirit Babies

The spirit of your baby is never alone. The angels always know when it is time for babies to make their transition. They come to lovingly guide and support each spirit during the journey. The angels also provide love and support as the spirit babies play and enjoy their time on the other side.

The Twins and Carolyn: Glowing Little Cherubs

Carolyn and Anthony were excited when they received the news they were pregnant with twins—then heartbroken when at eight weeks, Carolyn miscarried for no apparent medical reason. The devastating loss was compounded by the fact that Carolyn was already forty years old, had no children, and desperately wanted a baby.

I had just lost the twins, and was having a surgical procedure following the miscarriage. I was in that medically induced twilight state when I was given a wonderful vision. Two angels presented themselves to me. They appeared as human beings (one male and one female) about thirty years old, with brown, wavy hair that had a golden cast to it. Somehow they seemed to be like a mother angel and a father angel. They stood right next to the surgical table, but nobody else seemed to notice they were present. They didn't give me any messages, but I felt incredible love and support flowing from them.

I could also see lots and lots of baby angels behind my head. They were little naked cherubs with white wings, flying around and having fun. There was no end to the number of baby angels. The stream of glowing little cherubs flowed out as far as I could see. I knew they came to help the spirits of my twins cross to the other side.

It was such a magical vision! In that moment I felt so blessed to know my spirit babies were being taken care of by this family of angels. For the first time since the babies had left, I felt a deep sense of peace.

Angels Provide Protection to Family Members

When a baby is in crisis, angels provide support, love and protection to not only the baby, but also the devastated family members and anyone else affected by the situation. This assistance takes place even if those involved are not conscious of it, but it is more rewarding to be aware of the presence of angels and their healing energy. Recognizing angelic miracles always brings increased comfort and peace and a deeper feeling of being loved.

Harrison and Sharon: In the Arms of an Angel

Harrison spent four months in the NICU and his mother, Sharon, spent the whole time sitting beside his bed. Often she went without sleep for days.

I feel blessed because I have the ability to feel the presence of angels. One night Harrison was having trouble, so I was determined to stay up with him all night. Spirit, however, had other ideas for me. Early in the night a pair of warm, invisible arms picked me up and put me in the bed that was set up next to Harrison. For the first time in weeks I fell sound asleep, and didn't wake up until the next morning. I awoke so refreshed—it was a miracle.

I have always been able to feel spiritual energy more than I see it. I can sense that the angels are always around. I know God doesn't ever leave us alone. One day when Harrison was in the NICU, I said this prayer: "Harrison needs the angels more than I do, so don't put all of them on me."

Within seconds I felt small, vulnerable, exposed, and overwhelmed with fear. Immediately I thought, "I take it back. There are enough angels and divine love for everyone." I could really feel the difference as the angels surrounded me once again with their protection.

Harrison and Grandma Fran:
Angels Who Glimmer Like Tiny Stars

Grandma Fran also spent many days and nights with Harrison at the hospital. She was always uplifted by the presence of angels.

Angels are always around—it's just that most folks aren't aware of them. You see, angels are energy and so are we, but our human energy vibrates at a much slower rate; that's why you and I can see each other easily. In contrast, angels vibrate at such a high frequency that we can't usually see them with our human eyes. I have a natural gift of clairvoyance, so I can see and feel the spiritual energy of angels when I tune in to the spirit world.

I've had many experiences with angels throughout my life. One of the most unforgettable was having an angel protect me when I was in seventh grade. Two friends and I were walking home late at night when a man began stalking us. He looked very menacing, and we were terrified, thinking he might kill us. Suddenly, a huge golden light appeared, and surrounded all three of us. This golden angel stayed with us the whole way home, and actually lit our way in the dark. It was absolutely awesome! All three of us were very grateful, although we never spoke of it to anyone. In those days you just didn't talk about things of that nature.

I am so appreciative of my ability to sense different energies, and I continue to develop my skill. Often, when there is an angelic presence around, I see little tiny stars that shimmer down from heaven in a luminous stream. As a child I used to lie in bed at night and focus on the sparkling light. It always brought me comfort when I was afraid.

I see energy around people too. It looks like the shimmering that comes off the pavement on a hot summer day. I could always see this beautiful energy around my grandson Harrison. With my soul vision I could see that Harrison was enveloped in a huge bubble of radiant love energy, and within that, there was another bubble of energy that would change. Sometimes, it would be a brighter light, and other times it would be sparkling gold metallic or have a hint of turquoise. It was fascinating to watch, and I often wondered about the different colors.

When Harrison was sick, crossing the threshold of the NICU was like walking into a very spiritual world. I could always see thousands of tiny star-like glimmers, and the room was full of light. So, of course, I knew the room was full of angels protecting, loving, and nurturing the babies and all the worried family members who came to visit. Even though others couldn't see the light, they could perceive something was at work that was far beyond this physical world. Perhaps they, too, somehow sensed the room was filled with angels.

After four months in the NICU, Harrison began to grow weaker and weaker, and the doctors determined he would never be able to get off all the machines. I had a soul-to-soul dialogue with him, and got the message that he had made his choice. Harrison's soul had finished his life's work in those few months, and he was ready to go Home. I decided not to share this information with my daughter at that time. The human part of me was heartbroken, outraged, and fought the idea tooth and nail. My spiritual part, the compassionate, loving part of me, was blessing his decision. I was conflicted and in deep pain despite my advantage of seeing into the spiritual world.

The night my daughter and her husband made the decision to take Harrison off life support, I left the hospital around midnight. I was in so much pain knowing my dear Harrison would be leaving. The heartache seemed more than I could bear. All I could do was pray for assistance from Spirit. As I prayed, I felt a peaceful presence envelop me, and I knew without doubt that an angel came to be with me. I was surrounded with incredible divine love energy, and I could let go of everything—my fear, my anger and my heartache. It all just melted away. I didn't have to be strong any more. Just when I needed it the most, I was cradled in the energy of total peace and divine love. The feeling stayed with me all night long, and I know it will be in my heart forever.

I have peace about Harrison's transition. I believe he is always a part of everything around me—it's just the physical body that is not here. Having this spiritual connection allows me to be able to go on. Now Harrison is one of those star-like glimmers that I see with my spiritual senses!

Spirit Babies Act as Guardian Angels

After the death of an infant, the spirit baby stays connected to loved ones here on earth and often acts as a guardian angel for the family. These spirit babies are powerful healers, and they have the ability to create miracles when it is in divine order. Many times their protection gets attributed to "just being lucky."

Charles and Katie: Proof of Protection

I found myself mesmerized as Katie shared this story about receiving protection from Charles, her spirit baby.

Roses have always been my passion, particularly the variety known as the peace rose, so one spring I planted a peace rosebush. Sadly, as summer came and went, the bush never flourished. By fall, it looked totally dead, and I intended to dig it up and throw it away. However, I kept putting that chore off, so it was still in my rose garden when Charles Christopher was stillborn on November 6. I came home from the hospital, and found the most amazing sight. My dead rosebush had produced one exquisite rose!

This big, beautiful peace rose gave me a bit of hope in my deep sorrow. Roses don't bloom in Indiana in November, and they certainly don't bloom on a dead bush! This was indeed a miracle! I knew it was a sign from my son saying, "I'm in a better place—far better than this earth."

This rose stayed on the bush for some time. Then the bush went dormant again. As spring burst forth the following year, this bush produced another single peace rose—right in the same spot as the first one. Days later, a tornado touched down just two miles away, and these incredible high winds shredded all the roses in the garden—all but the lone peace rose! As I surveyed the damage around the neighborhood, I was incredulous that my home was left untouched. I know absolutely that Charles Christopher protected me through the storm, and the peace rose was his signature.

It's been almost six years, and Charles Christopher still sends me one precious peace rose each spring. This delicate sign brings me inner peace. My heart is filled with joy knowing my baby is still with me in spirit.

Dillon and Stephanie: Help From Heaven

Angels, spirits of our deceased loved ones, and even spirit babies often give a warning to people in the midst of danger when it is not their time to cross over. These warnings usually come through a sense of knowing as opposed to seeing or hearing anything specific.

Our baby Dillon lost his life before he could even come into the world, and I sank into a major depression, isolating myself from everyone. My grandfather wouldn't give up on me, and kept reaching out and sending the most precious notes. He seemed to always know what I needed and sent just the right words. I was amazed he could be so sensitive.

Shortly after Dillon's transition, my family organized a party for Grandpa's ninetieth birthday. I wasn't ready to socialize yet, but my husband, Mike, and I went to the party because my love for Grandpa was stronger than my need for privacy.

We were stopped at a red light on the way home. The light turned green, and for some unknown reason Mike didn't go through the light. We just sat there looking at each other. Then we both glanced to the left to see a car come barreling through the intersection.

The car behind us started honking, but we sat there in the dark, just absorbing the wonder of the moment. We both knew that if we had driven into that intersection three seconds earlier, we could have been killed! I said to Mike, "That was Dillon! I have no doubt about it!" He quickly agreed, though he is usually quite a skeptic. We both believe Dillon's spirit saved our lives that night.

Stephanie and Mike both had a knowing that their spirit baby inspired them to just sit at the light until the danger had passed. They didn't have to think about it—they just believed in that instant. This is exactly the way a knowing comes.

David and Patti: I Am Here to Help You

Patti has been on a spiritual path for many years. A surprising message came to her after taking classes to further her own spiritual development.

Soon after we married, my husband and I decided to take some spiritual classes. We were excited to learn about the unseen world and we loved improving our intuitive abilities. We began getting messages from angels, guides, and even loved ones on the other side. One day I felt a presence and decided to do some automatic writing.

After settling into a meditative state, I found myself writing, "I am David." Of course, when this came out of the blue I had no clue about the name David.

Next I wrote, "Who is this?"

The response that came through my pen blew me away, "This is your cousin who passed as an infant. I died from pneumonia. I'm here to help you. When you need me, say the Twenty-third Psalm."

I sat there stunned as the meaning of this message filtered into my mind. I had totally forgotten about David because I was only four when he died as a baby. At the time I didn't really understand much of what happened except I knew my mother was crying a lot. I remember asking my mom about him when I was eleven years old and she explained that he died of complications from pneumonia. When this spirit told me he died of pneumonia I knew it was really David—the infant who left our family years earlier.

So now in times of stress I call on the spirit of my infant cousin for guidance and assistance by saying these old familiar words as I go to sleep at night, "Yea, though I walk through the valley of the shadow of death...." I wake up the next morning knowing everything is going to be okay—and it is.

Here we see David sending powerful medicine to Patti just like the Inca spirit babies help heal mind, body, or spirit when they are called upon. Your baby who has transitioned to the other side is a powerful spiritual being who can also act as a healer for you. Feel free to express your love to your baby and, if you wish, ask for his or her help.

♥ ♥ ♥

Summary of Chapter Three

1) Angels are God's messengers of divine love. They remind us that our purpose here on earth is to give and receive unconditional love. They also help us learn how to do that.

2) Angels send subtle signs of their ever-loving presence. This sign may be a scent, a divinely guided synchronistic event, a dream, a daydream, or a physical sign such as a feather.

3) Angels appear in different forms to different people. They can show themselves in a myriad of ways—as beings in long, flowing white robes, as little cherubs with wings, as glimmering little stars, or as glowing lights with no form at all.

4) Angels take care of spirit babies, so your baby is never alone.

5) You can trust that your baby had angels guiding the way Home, and was then surrounded with love and support from the many angels who take care of spirit babies on the other side.

6) When a baby is in crisis, angels provide protection to both the baby and the worried family members.

7) Angels often work behind the scenes, so people often receive the benefit of their love and protection without being conscious of their presence.

8) Spirit babies sometimes show themselves as angels to their loved ones.

9) Your spirit baby is a powerful being who can also act as an angel and bring healing to you and your grieving family on earth.

10) Spirit babies are willing to assist loved ones on earth. You can pray to or simply talk with your baby in heaven for assistance any time you have a need.

CHAPTER FOUR

———— ❧ ————

Visitation Dreams

In my dreams you are alive and well,
Precious child, precious child.
In my mind, I see you clear as a bell,
Precious child, precious child.
—Karen Taylor-Good, Composer

Dreams are the most common form of spirit communication. This is so for several different reasons. First, your baby's spirit can "come through the veil" more easily while you're sleeping because it is a time when your mind is quiet and there is less resistance. Secondly, while your physical body requires sleep to rejuvenate each night, your spirit has no such need. Consequently, while you are sleeping, your spirit is free to leave your body and travel out into the universe. At such times, your spirit and your baby's spirit can meet. Sometimes when you awaken, you will remember these meetings as a dream. I call this experience a "dream visitation." Often, parents or other family members wake up after these dream visitations feeling loved and connected to their spirit baby and understandably, find this experience very comforting.

Ordinary Dreams vs. Visitation Dreams

It is important to distinguish between an ordinary dream and a visitation dream. An ordinary dream is often jumbled, confusing, and illusive. It quickly fades from memory unless you write it down. In contrast, a visitation dream usually resembles a vivid snapshot or video that is imprinted on your waking memory. In addition, dreamers frequently recall seeing intense, luminescent colors and a divine light that illuminates everything. One parent I was interviewing for this book described a dream and said, "I felt like I was really there in heaven with my baby." This is a common impression when remembering a visitation dream.

In some cases, dream visitations are a way for your infant to send you a loving message, much like those discussed in the previous chapters. At other times they are simply an opportunity for you and your beloved baby to spend one-on-one time with each other. Either way, once you are aware of the possibility, you will be prepared to recognize these wonderful visits when they occur. Chances are you will feel a renewed connection with your spirit baby and may even experience a profound healing as a result.

The following stories illustrate the power of visitation dreams and the various ways they bring healing to grieving loved ones.

A Dream as a Defining Moment

A dream can often open the door for you to make an instantaneous shift in your perspective about the loss of your infant. This shift sets the miracle of healing in motion.

Marley and Bernadette: I'm an Angel

Bernadette had a visitation dream that brought her peace in the midst of great sorrow. This dream was without a doubt a defining moment in her grief journey.

From the beginning of my pregnancy I had a sense that something was wrong. I was just starting to let go of that idea and feel comfortable when, at twenty weeks, the ultrasound showed Marley was developing without a brain. What a shock! The doctors gave us three choices: carry the baby to full term, induce labor now, or have the baby removed surgically. It was a terrible time, and I was struggling to find my way. Initially, I decided to go through with the surgery and made the arrangements. A few days later, I woke up and knew I had to see our beloved infant and hold her. I changed everything so I could be induced and then hold our baby.

A couple of nights before the procedure, Spirit gave me an amazing dream. In the dream I gave birth to a baby girl who was born perfect and whole. First she was an infant, and then in two seconds, she grew up and started walking, running, talking, and laughing. She was surrounded in light as she ran in circles around our home announcing, "I'm an angel! I'm an angel!" She was so happy and full of life!

I woke up from the dream and had my first moment of peace since receiving the terrible news. In the depths of my heartache I found an inner strength and thought, "I am going to be okay." I just know the thought came from my dream, and I'm forever grateful my baby could come to me with her healing message.

My parents, family, and friends were all very supportive; my mom even flew here to be with my husband and me through the procedure. She helped make the whole experience extremely beautiful. We each held Marley and then the three of us said a prayer together. My mom then took the tears from my eyes and gently placed them lovingly on Marley's little head. I truly believe I held an angel in that moment. How blessed I am!

Once again, we see the powerful outcome when a spirit baby acts as a healer. Bernadette awakened feeling uplifted and for the first time had a sense that she could heal from her tragedy. Hope bloomed in her heart when she saw Marley alive, whole, and happy in the spirit world.

All spirit babies appear whole in visions and dreams even if they were very sick or disabled during their physical lives. After a dream visitation loved ones are usually able to let go of worries about their baby continuing to suffer in the afterlife; this happens easily and effortlessly after seeing their precious little one alive and well in the spirit world. These dreams also provide strong support for believing in life after death, and thus open the door to an ongoing spiritual relationship with a beloved spirit baby. A visitation dream is not usually a total healing, but it can provide great hope and inspiration to grieving family members as they move forward on their journey.

Dreams Can Bring a Warning

It is very common for mothers, and sometimes fathers, to get a very subtle warning that their baby is not going to live. Often this warning comes in a dream. Most of the time parents ignore the message, because it is too painful to even contemplate. It is only in retrospect that they understand the dream came as gentle message to prepare them.

Starlet and Sylvia: God Softens the Blow

During our interview for this book Sylvia had an "Aha!" moment when she discovered the meaning of a dream she had while pregnant with her baby, Starlet.

About seven months into the pregnancy I started having very disturbing dreams. Mostly, I couldn't remember details, but I would wake up very upset. This went on for some time, yet I seem to have blocked all the details from my consciousness. But I had one very vivid dream that I want to share.

In this dream my daughter was alive, and she was so heavy I couldn't pick her up; no one else could either. My mom and dad, my fiancé, and my little sister—all the people who were regularly around me—were in the dream and nobody could pick her up. She was like dead weight.

This dream scared me even though at the time I didn't understand the meaning. I knew that dreams give cryptic messages that really mean something, but I didn't want to know why she was so heavy, so I spaced it out. I just now got the meaning when I said the words "dead weight." Actually, I forgot about these disturbing nightmares until just now when you asked me if I had any dreams!

Looking back, I can see these dreams were preparing me for the worst. It was God's way of softening the blow a bit. I believe my dream was a message from God, Star's soul, the angels, and my soul—all of them together were trying to make sure I was prepared.

Dreams That Tell Us About the Spirit World

Many grieving loved ones wonder what heaven is like after the loss of a baby. Of course, it's very difficult to find believable descriptions of the afterlife. Loved ones who report significant details of their dream visitations from beloved spirit babies provide us with the most viable descriptions of heaven.

The Twins and Marilyn: A Heavenly Roller Coaster

I met Marilyn several years after she miscarried twin boys very late in the pregnancy. She had this healing dream just two weeks after losing the babies.

The twins and I were in an amusement park. They looked exactly alike, with blondish brown hair and thin little faces. I guess they looked like their dad. I was standing on a grassy area watching them ride a roller coaster. I thought it was strange that my boys were already two years old. It seemed even stranger that they were riding a roller coaster at that age, but they were having such a wonderful time—and I was enjoying watching them. It was sort of all mixed up, yet it seemed very real to me. When they got off the ride, I was so happy to be with them and talk to them. We were all laughing together. I was happy and they were happy.

I woke up feeling like the whole scene actually happened. It gave me chills all over my body. It was so strange. First, I could still feel the joy of being with them. Then this deep sadness came over me because they weren't here. I guess I felt like it was something that should have been. They should have been alive, and I should have been able to enjoy being with them in a real amusement park.

The dream happened a year ago, but I still remember it in every detail. It's burned into my memory. It seemed true; of course, I hope it's true. I have different thoughts about that. Sometimes, I believe it was a message that my babies are happy and okay. Other times, I think my mind is just doing strange things. At times, I just think I'm nuts! So I go back and forth.

I was so excited to hear Marilyn's dream because the place she described matched what I had been told ten years earlier about a place on the other side called the Children's Plane. This information came from Margaret, a cancer client who crossed over and came back to speak with me through a spiritual medium named Roy Waite. Here is Margaret's description of a place she visited on one of her "field trips" through heaven.

Now I want to talk to you about a wonderful place called the Children's Plane. I love to go there because it is so beautiful, and filled with so much divine love. The spirit children who exist there are filled with joy because they live in this energy of unconditional love. In fact, everyone is joyful there. You just can't help but be filled with awe in such a place.

These planes of consciousness contain the wildest and most wonderful dreams a child could have. The spirit children are joyful when they discover the wonders of this realm. Each of them can wander endlessly, discovering one delightful treasure after another. It is a true fairyland!

You know, I always did love children when I was there on earth. I still do, so I often gather lots of spirit children around me. A lot of us have been working in the Children's Plane over here.

Marilyn's face filled with awe as I told her about Margaret and the Children's Plane. She felt honored that she had been given the gift of seeing her beloved twins in this place of joy and love. She said in amazement, "This information makes my dream even more special. I had no idea my dream was a spiritual experience."

Each sleep-time visitation is another reminder that our loved ones in Spirit, including our babies, want us to awaken to the joy and wonder that exists in their world. They keep sending dreams and other invitations, so we will open our soul senses and be aware of the beauty, peace, and love of the place where they now live. In this way your spirit baby sends powerful medicine to help soothe your heartache.

Meeting a Mother's Emotional Needs

Spirit babies are very aware of our emotions. Without interfering with our free will, they offer love, support, and healing messages. When they see us suffering the grief of losing them, spirit babies offer emotional support by letting us know that they still exist in a state of peace and joy, and that they wish the same for us.

Peter and Tracy: Breath on My Face

Peter was stillborn five days after his due date though no medical cause was ever found. Peter's mother, Tracy, held his lifeless body at the hospital yet she had deep yearnings for more physical contact with this baby who came into her life and left so abruptly. Her spirit baby was able to meet her needs in a unique dream visitation.

> *One night after our infant support group meeting I was very emotional. Other mothers were telling stories of their babies who were born alive. They had memories of their babies grasping their finger or cuddling with them in the NICU. I felt cheated that Peter never lived—he only lived inside of me. I interacted with him while he was in my womb. I sang to him, patted him, and felt his many movements. He, however, had no opportunity to interact with me, and I longed for just one more thing to remember him by. I needed him to know how much I loved him.*
>
> *That night I had a dream. Peter came to me and I actually felt his breath on my face. I had so much peace when I woke up. I felt so good! At first I didn't know what to think about it but I kept coming back to the peace I felt. I finally started believing he really did come to me—it was too real to be just a dream.*

Melissa and Heather: Red Curly Ringlets

Heather shared this dream about her spirit daughter Melissa—a powerful spirit who brought healing to her mother's deep fears.

When Melissa, my first-born, passed as an infant, I was so afraid I wouldn't have another baby. I worried about this all the time. When she was gone about a year I began praying, "I've got to have a sign about having another baby. Please send me a sign." I prayed about this every night for weeks. Finally, my prayers were answered with a very vivid dream.

I was standing in this vast green field that was filled with tiny wild flowers as far as I could see. The flowers were awesome, deep, rich colors. They were glowing—deep purple, yellow, pink, lavender, and even blue. The flowers were flowing back and forth though I felt no breeze. It was the most beautiful scene ever! When I looked up there was no sky—just bright white light everywhere.

Ahead was a huge oak tree with a rope swing hanging from a big branch. There was a little girl with long brown hair in a long white dress swinging on the swing. She looked just like Melissa except she was about five years old. I walked right up to her and hugged her up saying, "Are you okay?" She answered, "Mama, I'm fine." My heart flew open with joy and love!

A little boy was sitting in the grass near the swing wearing a white John-John suit. He had this mass of red curly hair—red ringlets everywhere. He was the cutest thing I ever saw! I walked over to him and asked, "Who are you?" He just smiled at me. Melissa said, "You aren't supposed to know who he is yet."

This sense of wonder filled me as I woke. This dream was different from regular dreams because it was so intense, and everything was so vibrant. I know I was standing right there in heaven with my babies—one from the past and another one from the future. My arms were aching to hold another baby and here was Melissa, my spirit daughter, telling me that my arms would soon be filled. This was Melissa's way of letting me know she was okay and that I would be okay.

This was great news and I wanted to spread it. I was so excited that I told anybody who would listen about this dream. My mother totally believed me. Of course, I thought she would because our whole family is into believing we get signs through dreams. Some people outside the family believed me, and some thought I was kind of crazy. That didn't matter because I wasn't looking for approval—I just wanted to share my joy.

Several months later, I found out I was pregnant with a boy; we named him Cameron. I never once worried that something would happen with this pregnancy. The whole time I knew this baby was going to be the little boy in my dream. When he was born the first thing I saw was this full head of curly red hair! Amazing!

I have a picture of Cameron in a little white suit at two years old—he is the exact image of the little boy in my dream. The picture reminds me that my son existed in some form a full year before he came to me as a baby. I feel extremely grateful and privileged to have met my child before even conceiving him. Looking at that picture fills me with awe!

Interpreting Dreams So They Heal

Just having a dream visitation from your infant's spirit does not automatically mean it will be a healing experience for you. If you dismiss this event as "just a dream," or let others—or even your own rational mind—convince you a visit with your spirit infant simply is not possible, you might miss the opportunity for healing. Your awareness of the event and your ability to acknowledge its spiritual significance make an important contribution to the effect it will have on you.

Diana and Ruth: Rocking Together in Heaven

Ruth came to me seeking help for severe depression that started after the loss of her baby. In our first session, she reported a recurring dream about Diana, her beautiful baby girl who was stillborn.

For six months after Diana died, I had this dream several times each week. It was very disturbing and I still don't know what to make of it. I would dream that I was sitting in a rocking chair holding Diana. There were never any words—just the rocking.

In the dream Diana is wrapped in a pink blanket, and she has that peaceful contented look that babies get. I can see both of us as if I'm watching from across the room. I notice that I look peaceful too—I am so happy to be rocking my baby girl. I also see a sort of misty light around us as we rock together.

Each time after the dream, I would wake up and think for a time that Diana was still alive. Then reality would hit me, and my grief would be ten times worse.

> *I was afraid to tell anybody about these dreams—even my husband*
> *still doesn't know. Finally I shared them with my best friend. She*
> *told me they were not healthy, and I should pray for them to stop.*
> *She was really upset and told me it was all happening because I*
> *wasn't getting over Diana's death. I felt really terrible after that, so*
> *I never told anyone else. But the dreams continued for months.*

Notice how Ruth describes the experience as disturbing, yet she also says both she and her daughter were peaceful during the dream. Sadly, she was unable to bring the feeling of peace into her waking life. Ruth shifted from peace to grief because she focused on yearning to have her baby back as opposed to keeping her thoughts centered on the love and peace of the visitation.

Ruth looked at me with awe when I explained that her connection with Diana in this dream is evidence of the eternal love bonds within a family. She was shocked when I explained that Diana's spirit was coming through dreams to help her heal her grief. The misty light around the two of them was a clue that they were meeting in a place of very wonderful spiritual energy—a place of light. I told her that they both needed this time to be together, quietly rocking and enjoying one another's presence, to share their love in the spirit world.

Ruth listened intently as I shared my spiritual understanding of what's happening when we dream about deceased loved ones—including babies. After a quiet moment she said, "I wish I'd known that my baby was coming to help me heal. That never occurred to me. I missed the message completely."

The Twins and Larry: Tossing a Ball

Larry began to have a recurring dream after his wife, Darlene, miscarried their twin boys. Every two or three months for a period of about five years, Larry dreamed that he and the twins were in a golden field, tossing a football back and forth. That was it—they just tossed the ball to one another. From the beginning, the boys did not look like little babies, but rather like youngsters about four or five years old.

Because the dreams were so simple and the boys' actions seemed so mundane, Larry saw little spiritual meaning in them. He was always very nonchalant about discussing these dreams, even with Darlene. One time he commented to his wife, "It's just a dream."

Darlene, on the other hand, was quite excited about her husband's dreams. She saw them as affirmation that there is an afterlife and that the twins still exist in the spirit world.

Darlene and Larry were viewing his dreams through very different eyes. Darlene chose to see them through her soul eyes, which brought her comfort and healing for her grief. In contrast, Larry saw the dreams through his human eyes and put little spiritual value on them. Consequently, he did not receive much comfort or healing.

Jean Margaret and Dr. Jessica:
The Heart and Soul of a Physician

Dr. Jessica loves babies and devotes much of her time as a family practice physician to taking care of pregnant women and their babies. She believes this work is a calling from her soul. Dr. Jessica had an enlightening dream after delivering a stillborn baby girl.

One of the most powerful events in my medical career took place during the first year of my practice. I was the attending physician for the stillbirth of a beautiful baby girl. I will never, ever, in my whole life forget—never, ever. It still touches my heart, and I will remember this little baby and her family forever!

The birth of Jean Margaret demanded that I be present for her parents, Nancy and David, in such a deep way. They needed more than just a physician attending to the physical challenges of their baby; they needed what I could give from the deepest part of me— my heart and soul.

A few days before her due date, Nancy called me saying, "My baby's not moving." Immediately, I sent her to the hospital and arranged to meet her there. The initial ultrasound showed no heartbeat, and I had to confirm what this mother already knew. "She's gone. I'm so sorry." Nancy, David, and I were all crying together for quite a while. It was heart wrenching.

After doing Nancy's C-section, I went home at three o'clock in the morning. I was devastated. I prayed and prayed for this family. Of course, I began to wonder, "What did I miss? Maybe I'm not meant for this. Maybe this work with babies takes more than I have."

That same night, I dreamed I was in the operating room and again delivered Jean Margaret as a stillborn. As I placed her on the warmer and stood there looking at her, David came walking through the door holding the hand of a little girl with curly, light brown hair. I knew immediately this was Jean Margaret presenting herself as an older child. She was clearly disabled with cerebral palsy and was profoundly affected; her eyes were vacant and her face muscles were lax.

Still standing over the baby's body, I looked at the dad and the little girl and asked, "Was there anything I could have done?" Jean Margaret looked up at me, and for a moment, her eyes were alert and in perfect focus. "Zero," she said. I immediately understood her message; there was nothing I could have done to save her. She was also telling me that, had she lived, she would not have been a normal child.

Despite the dream, I went through hell! I had a lot of guilt—I even did some counseling to help me with these feelings. Logically, it made no sense that I was feeling responsible for the loss of this baby. The autopsy came back indicating that Jean Margaret's umbilical cord was malformed and was unable to deliver enough oxygen for her brain to develop normally. Obviously not my fault.

During the pregnancy, we had performed all the usual testing, but there was never any indication that the cord was abnormal. For whatever reasons, it seems we were not supposed to know.

All this clinical information helped me think more clearly about why this baby died. However, her death and my grief were matters of the heart—and all these facts just couldn't touch that deeper part of me. I had to heal my wounded heart by releasing my grief and dealing with my feelings of being helpless to save her. I already knew in my head that some things are just meant to be, and there's nothing you can do to change them. With the loss of Jean Margaret, I understood this lesson with my heart.

In a strange sort of way, the autopsy brought me some peace because it confirmed what my soul told me in the dream. Had this baby lived, she would have been profoundly disabled because of brain damage. My soul-self got the message long before my human-self. And strangely, the mother was the first to know! Throughout the pregnancy, Nancy kept saying, "There's something wrong with my baby." And she was right. Never again will I discount a mother's intuition!

Bryce and Lori: A Little Glimpse of Heaven

One evening just ten days before her due date, Lori told her husband, Toby, that their baby wasn't moving very much. She wasn't too concerned because she thought it was normal for babies to move less near delivery time and had experienced this with their first-born son. The next day she went for her regular checkup, expecting her doctor to tell her not to worry. Instead, she heard, "I'm so sorry. I can't find your baby's heartbeat." In shock and hardly able to comprehend what was happening, Lori and Toby were sent to the hospital. After laboring for eight hours that night, Lori delivered a perfectly formed, stillborn baby boy. She and Toby chose to name their infant son Bryce.

This catastrophic event catapulted Lori into shock, deep, agonizing grief, and a healing journey that took three years. She had several dream experiences that were pivotal to healing her agonizing heartache.

Just one week after Bryce was stillborn, I had a vivid dream about him. In the dream he appears to be three or four years old, and I'm observing him from a distance, as if I'm looking through a window. He's in a meadow filled with high grass. A gentle breeze is blowing the grass and wild flowers back and forth. The sun is shining—like luminescent, bright. Strangely, there is no sound—it's like I'm watching a movie with the sound turned off.

I see my son kneeling down a little to smell some flowers. I'm looking at his profile and see that his pretty, straight, shiny, brownish-blonde hair is touched with the sun. That's all. The dream is just me observing my son in this beautiful environment with the sun glowing.

When I woke up, I thought, "Oh isn't that sweet!" For a few minutes, I wondered if that's what Bryce would have looked like at the age of three or four if he'd lived. I let the dream go without much thought; it just seemed logical to dream about our baby who had just died.

Then, two years after losing our infant son, I attended a weekend workshop where I had a transformational healing experience. While in a group meditation (very much like a dream state), this translucent, sparkly-blue energy came towards me and stayed fluttering around me for several minutes. It reminded me of Tinker Bell, but then I realized it was the spirit of our infant son. So I started talking to him, saying, "Hi, Sweetie. How are you? I love you so much."

At that very moment, the facilitator asked the whole group, "What are you afraid of?" At first, I thought, "Nothing." Then this answer came from somewhere deep within, "When my time comes to cross over, what if I find out I was to blame for my baby's death?" Suddenly my whole being was filled with fear and overwhelming guilt. These feelings had previously pricked my consciousness, but I would never allow them to come to the fore. That whole subject had always been too devastating to even contemplate.

This little ball of blue energy kept dancing around me as I allowed the guilt and fear to wash over me. Then those negative feelings simply evaporated (Poof!), and the energy of my son's love permeated every cell of my being. I was filled with a deep peace, a peace I'd never felt before.

After I shared my story with the group, the facilitator said, "Now that you've let go of the guilt, you have an empty space. What are you going to fill it with?" I answered immediately, "I'm going to fill it with more love for my child and more love for myself. And I'm going to fill it with a mission to help others who are suffering after losing an infant." For the first time in my life, I knew my spiritual mission.

A year later, I was asked to be the guest speaker at a memorial service for families in grief after infant death. It took a lot for me to go because it had only been a few weeks since delivering my fourth baby by C-section. My abdomen was in excruciating pain after taking a fall that injured my incision. I feared I wouldn't even be able make it through the service, let alone give a speech. But I was determined to go no matter how much my body hurt. So I went.

The service was beautiful, filled with so much comfort for all of us who had experienced infant loss. When I finished my speech, I sat back down, and the chaplain began speaking. He said, "If you ever have a dream of your baby, and he seems to be older, and he's in a field somewhere with the sun shining down, I want you to know that is not a dream. That is a glimpse of your child in heaven."

This chaplain had just described my dream! I sat there immobilized! I remember thinking, "Did I just hear that?" All of a sudden this simple dream from three years before took on a huge meaning for me. The scenes in the dream flashed through my mind once again. This time I saw that the luminescent light—like no light I had ever seen before—filled everything. I became aware that the light was coming from inside the flowers and inside my son. Everything was lit with a light from within as opposed to a light from without. Slowly it dawned on me that what I'd been calling "sunlight" was really the light of God!

When I left the church that day, I was healed both physically and emotionally. It was like somebody flipped a switch, and the pain from my C-section simply evaporated and never came back. In a moment of grace, all my remaining heartache simply melted away and was replaced with feelings of love and peace. I was healed on many levels once I understood that I had truly seen my child in heaven.

Inviting a Dream Visitation

If you have not yet had a dream visitation, you can be proactive and send an invitation to the spirit of your beloved infant. These seven steps are designed to create a state of readiness and increase the possibility of having a visitation from your baby.

1) Allow yourself to relax in bed before going to sleep. Set aside your grief for the moment and focus on the love you have for your spirit baby.

2) Visualize divine love energy flowing into the top of your head and filling all your cells, as well as your heart space.

3) Write a letter of intention to your spirit baby stating your desire to connect with him or her. Stay positive and affirm that you are open to a dream visit. It might look like this:

   Dear Spirit Baby, it is my intention to have a dream visitation with you tonight while I'm sleeping. I expect to easily and effortlessly remember the experience when I awaken.

4) Place your journal or a writing tablet next to your bed, so you can record the highlights of your dream experience.

5) Move into a state of thankfulness and appreciation for this opportunity to connect with your baby's spirit.

6) Allow yourself to drift off to sleep.

7) Write down the dream experience immediately upon waking.

These seven steps will open the door for a dream visitation. Be gentle with yourself and your baby's spirit if your visit doesn't occur immediately. Trust that, because you are asking, it will happen in divine order with perfect timing. I invite you to repeat these steps each night, and keep a positive expectation that your baby will indeed come to share time while you sleep. Enjoy your visit!

♥   ♥   ♥

Summary of Chapter Four

1) Dreams are the most common form of spirit communication.

2) While sleeping, your spirit is free to leave your body, travel out into the universe, and spend time with your spirit baby. Upon awakening, the experience feels very real. This experience is a dream visitation.

3) Visitation dreams are vivid, filled with intense luminescent colors or divine light, and imprinted on your waking memory. They are very different from ordinary dreams.

4) A visitation dream is often a defining moment on your healing journey. It can shift your perspective about life after death and set healing in motion.

5) Visitation dreams sometimes bring a subtle warning that a baby is not going to live. This message is usually ignored because it is too painful to contemplate.

6) Spirit babies can come in dreams and provide viable descriptions of heaven. They want us to awaken to the joy and wonder that exists in their world.

7) How you interpret a dream affects your ability to receive healing from the experience.

8) Grieving loved ones sometimes miss the message of a visitation dream and, consequently, lose an opportunity to heal.

9) Spirit babies act as healers for their loved ones when they appear in dreams. They can provide the opportunity to heal the emotional needs of everyone involved.

10) You can be proactive and use visualizations to increase the possibility of having a visitation from your spirit baby.

CHAPTER FIVE

———— ❧ ————

Eternal Family Love Bonds

*One of the most consistent facts of the spirit world
is that spirits leap at every opportunity to be seen
and heard, and children, with their heightened,
unedited psychic senses, provide some
of the best opportunities.*
—*Sylvia Browne, Psychic and Author*

Most people believe in some form of afterlife for the spirits of their deceased loved ones. After the loss of an infant, grieving family members usually begin to wonder about the nature of this place where the spirit of their baby now resides. I interviewed members of numerous families who had lost an infant, and they asked these common questions: *"Is my baby alone and lost in an unfamiliar place?" "Who is taking care of my baby?" "Does the spirit of my baby feel my love?"*

Loved ones often yearn for believable answers to these very important questions. This collection of stories provides evidence that the spirit of your deceased infant stays connected to family on both sides of the veil. Indeed, you will see that the bonds of family love stretch into eternity and are never broken. Hopefully, this will bring you great comfort and reassurance.

I invite you to see that the spirit babies in these stories act as healers for their families and loved ones. They send powerful medicine for healing grief after the loss of an infant, just as the Inca spirit babies at Pachatusan.

Spirit Babies Communicate With Young Children

All across the globe, it is quite common for young children to report seeing the spirit of a deceased infant. Some also report having conversations with the baby's spirit. These accounts from young children are significant because they are spontaneous and unsolicited. Consequently, they have a decided ring of truth. I believe the spirits of deceased infants can come through to these young children because they have not been conditioned to doubt or resist the supernatural. While visiting infant loss support groups,

I interviewed many grieving parents who shared stories of young children receiving spirit communication from infants who had crossed over.

One father, who lost a baby girl, saw his three-year-old daughter lying in bed at nap time staring at the ceiling. When he asked her what she was staring at, she responded, "My baby sister. She's right there."

Another mother, who lost a baby named Gabriel, reported this scenario: "We were all in the kitchen getting ready for dinner, and our four-year-old seemed to be staring at something I couldn't see. When I asked him about this, he answered, 'I'm watching Baby Gabriel.'"

After losing her baby daughter Alison, Holly prayed every night for the baby's spirit to come to her in a dream. This mother never received a visitation, but after the third night her five-year-old son spontaneously announced, "Alison was in my dream last night!" He could remember all the details and shared them with his mother. Holly was thrilled to know that her daughter's spirit came for a visit and sent a message through her son. It was a moment of great joy!

New Baby and Michelle: Bye-Bye, Baby

Michelle is a midwife who is quite intuitive and very connected to babies and young children. She shared this delightful story with me.

My son Brandon was two years old and talking quite clearly. I was three months pregnant and had talked to him about the "baby in my tummy." He was so excited that a new baby was joining our family.

One day, I was rocking quietly and nursing my son when he popped off the breast, looked up above my head, and called out, "Bye-bye, Baby."

I laughed and responded, "Where did the baby go?"

He replied in a singsong voice, "Way up high."

At the time, it seemed like we were playing a sweet little game; however, three days later I began to spot and the pregnancy ended in a miscarriage. I'm sure my baby's spirit left at the moment my son said, "Bye-bye, Baby." It just took three days for this leaving to come to pass at the physical level. I'm filled with awe every time I think of Brandon announcing our baby's transition to the spirit world! It was such a sacred moment!

Four months later, I became pregnant again and Brandon announced, "It's a girl!" He was right! This little boy of mine certainly seems to know what's going on with the babies who are coming to join the family.

Elyse and Laurie: A Loving Goodbye

Laurie, a respiratory therapist, attended one of my psychic development workshops. She gifted me with this story just days before this book went to press. In fact the book was already typeset, but my intuition said to hold the press because this story was important. So here's Laurie's story as she told it to me.

Elyse, our first-born, was quite a precocious communicator. When she was only four months, we taught her to sign, and she learned to speak very early, using phrases and short sentences at eight or nine months. She was speaking quite clearly at fourteen months when this remarkable incident occurred.

I was very tired and laid down with Elyse for her afternoon nap. I dozed off, but was awakened by an infant's cry. Elyse was wide awake next to me, patting my stomach and kissing my belly, but she was too old to cry like a baby. I was mystified.

I asked her, "What are you doing?" "Baby," she responded. I laughingly replied, "There's no baby." Elyse looked at my belly again and said, "Baby, bye-bye. It's okay. I love you." She continued to kiss and pat my belly while repeating, "I love you. I love you."

Not knowing what to make of her behavior, I picked her up in my arms saying, "Come now. Let's go back to sleep," and we both fell sound asleep for a long nap. When I woke up, I found myself wondering, "Did that really happen? Was that a dream? Who was she talking to?"

Two weeks later I started cramping severely, so I went to my doctor, who gave me the shock of my life when he said, "You're having a miscarriage. I believe you're about twelve weeks pregnant." Then I remembered what Elyse was doing that afternoon and understood that somehow she knew her unborn baby brother or sister was in my belly, and that they had been telling each other goodbye. How awesome! What a miracle!

Elyse never mentioned this incident again. I often wonder if she remembers speaking with this soul we never got to meet. She didn't seem to mourn for this baby even though my husband, Charles, and I grieved deeply. It hurt us a lot! It was a real loss for us because we started our family late and truly wanted more children. We shed many, many tears, spent hours talking about our little one who didn't make it into this world, and did a lot of praying to heal our grief.

Soon after, we had two more miscarriages, but Elyse didn't seem to notice. Then we were gifted with a healthy baby girl and later, a beautiful baby boy. We feel so blessed! Even though my husband and I had three children we never held, we both believe we will be with these spirit babies when we go to heaven. What a joyful meeting that will be!

Lane and Heather: He Flies With Us

Heather, "Mom to three angels," contributed this sweet story illustrating communication from a spirit baby to an earthly sibling.

I have an extra sense; my mother and grandmother have it too. Apparently, my two living boys are intuitive like us, and they have had some spiritual experiences at tender ages.

When Cameron was young he told me he was awake in my womb. He said it like this, "Mama, I could open my eyes inside you, but it was dark. So Jesus held me and would sing to me and tell me I would be okay, 'cause he knew I was scared of the dark. Yes, Mama, it happened!" Now, he said this so sincerely and very matter of fact, so I have to believe him.

My Cameron was nine years old and Christopher (better known as C.J.) was five years old when Lane died as a newborn in the NICU. They were so looking forward to having another brother to play with, and they still miss him really hard. They don't grieve all the time, but they are aware of missing him and still feel connected to him.

In fact, C.J. talks about his baby brother quite often—apparently, he talks with him too! He frequently tells me how happy Lane is. One day, C.J. announced out of the blue, "Lane likes fire trucks." Another time, he said, "Do you know Lane is thinking about you today?" Once, he even gave me a present saying, "Lane told me to get this for you." We were outside on a sunny day, and C.J. was picking up rocks and feathers and putting them in a box when he casually announced, "Lane likes rocks and feathers." C.J. collects them all the time now and takes them to the cemetery when we go visit Lane's gravesite.

It's become evident that C.J. is also able to see spirits. At age three he saw Uncle Raymond sitting on the porch swing just hours after this beloved uncle died at the hospital. Of course, I could see nothing.

When C.J. was eight years old, he drew me a picture and said, "This is Lane with angel wings. He flies with us everywhere we go." I was overjoyed to hear this news about my sweet baby. It is very comforting to know he's so close. These little announcements from my son always warm my heart. I believe babies open the door to heaven!

Carlos and Victoria: Cali, Come Play With Me!

Victoria and I met at an international conference about healing the grief of losing an child. She is from South America and traveled all the way to the United States searching for assistance to ease her devastating heartache. She was delighted to share her sweet story, and I'm delighted to share it with you.

Our little boy, Carlos, had a best friend named Oliver who lived across the street. Oliver was a bright two year old who spoke very clearly for his age. The two boys were the only children on the block so they played together often. Little Oliver couldn't pronounce Carlos, so he called our son "my friend Cali." This sweet little neighbor boy came across the street almost every day to play with Carlos.

These two boys loved each other and were very connected— actually, they seemed more like brothers than neighborhood friends. Oliver had a little boy doll that he also called Cali. He carried it everywhere and wouldn't go to sleep without it. The doll was his security blanket. If Cali was missing, it became a household crisis until the toy was found.

Our dear sweet Carlos was sixteen months old when he drowned in our little plastic swimming pool. We had a fence around it, but somehow the gate was open, and he slipped out of our sight for just a few moments. That's all it took for tragedy to strike. It happened about 4:30 on a Sunday afternoon. We were devastated and inconsolable.

Oliver's family came to the funeral home for the wake. Oliver carried a bouquet of flowers; as he presented it to me, he said, "These are from Cali and me. We love you very much." I was so surprised!

My grief was overwhelming—for the first few months, I could hardly get out of bed each day. I had no visits or messages from my son; but then, I didn't really believe in such things.

A year after our Carlos drowned, Oliver's mother, Marie, came and told me the most intriguing story. It changed my whole grief experience. Here is this fascinating account in Marie's words:

> *I was outside in the back yard planting rose bushes in our garden that Sunday morning before Carlos drowned in the pool. For a time, Oliver played around me—even digging for a while with his little shovel. We went in for lunch about noon and I put Oliver down for his nap. I couldn't find his doll, but strangely, Oliver never uttered a peep about missing Cali and went to sleep without it.*
>
> *Surprisingly, Oliver never asked for it again. So finally, four days later, I asked Oliver, "Where is your doll, Cali?"*
>
> *Oliver said nonchalantly, "Oh, he's gone. He will never come back."*
>
> *So I asked, "Well, where did he go?"*
>
> *Oliver announced, "I will show you."*
>
> *With that, he took me by the hand, led me out to the rose garden, and showed me where he had buried his doll at the edge of the rose garden.*
>
> *Looking at the ground, he said, "He's going to stay here forever."*
>
> *I was mystified when I realized that my son had buried his toy sometime Sunday morning—hours before Carlos drowned in the pool.*
>
> *I became even more mystified over the next weeks. Each night, I would put Oliver to bed, kiss him goodnight, and turn out the lights. Soon, I would hear Oliver laughing and running around the bedroom.*
>
> *One night, I secretly listened by the door and, amidst my son's laughter, I heard, "Oh, Cali! Come and play with me! Come here. Give me that car."*

I quietly opened the door and looked in, but I couldn't see my son's invisible playmate. Your spirit son Carlos came to play quite often for the first ten months. He still comes, but not quite so often anymore.

As Marie finished her story, we hugged, and laughed and cried together. It was such a healing for me! She was thrilled at my reaction. Marie shared with me that she kept this beautiful story a secret because she thought it would hurt me somehow.

After hearing this story, my heart was so happy for my baby and I wept tears of joy. Finally, I had some peace. I don't really know, but I believe there is something beyond this life here. One thing I know for sure, my Carlos is happy where he is!

Knowing that our son comes to play with Oliver has brought me great freedom from my grief. The biggest change for me was that my anger with God just dissolved. For a whole year, I had been so angry with God. I even decided God didn't exist.

Miraculously, this story about a little doll opened my heart and I let God back in. I now believe God loves me. I also believe I have a direct line from me to God because I'm connected to my son in Spirit.

Miracle and Kahlilia: I Saw Her in My Dream

Kahlilia experienced a deep depression after the death of her infant daughter, Miracle. The uplifting memory of a butterfly message was very precious but wasn't enough to completely alleviate her despair. She prayed for a sign, a message, or a dream, and her prayers were answered in quite a surprising way.

Brianna, my goddaughter, and I were very close. She was six years old when I was expecting, and she was so anticipating the birth of my little baby girl. Brianna was crushed when I lost the baby and we cried a lot together. I soon began to withdraw; I isolated myself from people, even from Brianna, during my deepest grief. About eight months after Miracle's transition, I had a fascinating phone conversation with my sweet and wise goddaughter.

Brianna called and began, "I miss you, Kahlilia. How are you doing?"

I answered, "I'm doing okay."

Then she said the most unusual thing, "Miracle is okay, too. I saw her in my dream and I was talking to her."

Immediately I felt a sense of relief. It was such a gift to know my daughter was okay in Spirit and could appear to her godsister. I hadn't felt so much comfort since Miracle made her transition.

It was easy for me to believe that my goddaughter really had this dream because I knew Brianna had the gift of communicating with spirits. Her grandfather died when she was only four years old. Weeks later, she announced, "I'm not scared to sleep in my room now. Pop-Pop said he would protect me. Now I don't have to be afraid of the dark anymore."

Brianna has continued to have dream visits from my daughter, and I'm so thankful to get the messages through her. Knowing Miracle is around helps soothe my sorrow. Brianna is always so matter-of-fact when she talks about these visits. It's just everyday, normal life to her. I'm sure she believes everybody has these spirit dreams.

Cynthia and Marilyn: A Playmate for My Daughters

Marilyn and her husband Tom were bereft when Cynthia, their first-born, died of SIDS at two months. They both tried to bury their grief, hoping it would simply heal with time. When Cynthia died, Marilyn didn't believe in life after death; her philosophy was, "When you're dead, you're dead." To this day, she is in total amazement regarding this event that unfolded eight years after their precious Cynthia went to heaven.

My girls Shelley, age five, and Alison, age four, gave me the shock of my life one day when they came upstairs from the playroom and announced, "We need three sets of silverware and dishes to put in our basket. We are playing picnic with our new little friend, Cynthia." My heart did a flip, and I had to sit down before I fell down.

Cynthia was a family secret. The girls were born three years and four years after Cynthia died. Tom and I made a decision never to tell them about their older sister. It seemed so unfair to burden them with our grief and this sad story. Besides, my husband and I couldn't ever talk about our first baby without breaking down. So we put away all her pictures and erased every trace of her existence. Our plan was to tell the girls "someday" when they were older.

My daughter Shelley casually announced, "Cynthia comes to play a lot. She said she's our sister. We have so much fun together. She laughs a lot."

Imagine my shock! I couldn't think, talk, or make sense of what my daughter was telling me! In a word, I was completely freaked out!

Since that dramatic moment, I've learned that spirit babies sometimes show up as playmates to young children in the family. It's been a big awakening, but I do believe this little visitor is our spirit daughter, and it does my heart good to know she is connected to her sisters. I think of Cynthia as an invisible playmate, but she certainly is not invisible to my girls.

Five Spirit Siblings and Kathleen: Family Photos

Kathleen was raised in a big Irish immigrant family; in fact, she was the first one of the family to be born in America. Now in her fifties, Kathleen remembers growing up in a multi-generational family home and spending her childhood with her grandparents and great-grandparents, as well as numerous aunts, uncles, great aunts, and great uncles. The Old Irish often made comments about seeing the dead and talking with them. Kathleen was also born with "the gift"—meaning, like her great-grandfather and her grandmother, she could see and hear spirits. Kathleen shared these sweet stories about interacting with her spirit siblings.

My mother absolutely loved babies! She was happiest when she was holding one of her own or making over a neighbor's baby. My parents had six single births and then a set of twin boys; sadly, three of these children died as toddlers, and then the twins died as newborns. Mother almost died in childbirth with the twins, and she never really got over their deaths.

I was the oldest of the bunch, and since I had the gift, my five siblings were never really dead to me—they appeared and disappeared quite regularly in my daily life. One of my little brothers died when I was only three. Although I have no memory of this, my great-grandfather always told the story of "catching me questioning the air" soon after my brother's death. I was forever asking my spirit brother questions about what ancestors he'd met on the other side. I'd tell Grandpa, "He's safe. He's happy. Don't worry. He met your sister who just went to heaven."

My mother didn't want to hear stories of my conversations with my brothers and sisters on the other side. She seemed to think it was all wishful thinking on my part. One evening, Mom got very upset when I wanted to set a place at the dinner table for my dead brother. After that, I stopped telling her about their visits. That was a closed door, but we were very close. Looking back, it's very sad she wouldn't let me help her with her grief.

The three toddlers would often show up in my great-grandfather's garden when I was working in my little plot. Funny thing, they each came alone to visit me and have our little conversations. They seemed to keep growing up like kids do here on earth—they got older as I got older. I only talked about them to my great-grandfather because they came to him, too.

The visits from the twins were very different from those of my other brothers and my sister. The spirit twins seemed to hang out more in the background, and they didn't talk much. I always waited for them to get their voices, but that never happened. They seemed to relate more to our ancestors in heaven than to the relatives here on earth. When grandpa died, they told me, "We are very happy to have grandpa with us. We're sharing time with him and getting to know him." After that, I always looked at death as sharing!

We had lots of family parties, and my five spirit siblings all showed up whenever we gathered the children together for a family photo. This was the only time they appeared together. I could see all five of them taking their places between the cousins as some aunt or uncle tried to organize the kids. Immediately, I would start directing them saying, "Move over there so they can see you. Don't hide behind Eileen." I always thought the pictures would prove they were really present. I wanted the rest of the family to see what I was seeing. Of course, that never happened. My mother never understood that I was talking to my spirit siblings at these times—she just thought I was being really bossy to my living cousins. I still have two of these family photos from my childhood, and it always warms my heart to look at them.

The Twins and Sophia: Holding Hands Across the Veil

Sophia gave birth to four babies in three years, including a set of identical twin girls, Carolyn and Vanessa. Sophia showed me a picture of her daughters, both with big blue eyes and the same sweet, adorable expression on their faces; it was taken just weeks before Vanessa died of SIDS at the age of four months. Sophia was misty eyed, yet calm as she described her healing journey for the past seven years. Here is her story.

I've always had a different understanding about death, and I believed from my own experiences that death was not final. Since early childhood, I knew spirits were around.

I was twenty years old when my grandmother died. I could actually see her spirit at her funeral; she hovered around the casket and then floated through the church. Nobody could see her but me—at least no one mentioned it. She stayed around for three days and then she left. It was very comforting to know she was still "alive" and this recognition brought an inner peace, although my heart still ached because I could never hug her again.

I also saw my father's spirit for months after he made his transition, so I knew he was alive and well in Spirit. It was a blessing that he wasn't entirely gone from my life.

Little did I know these experiences were preparing me for the most devastating night of my life. All the children were sleeping upstairs and, for the first time since the twins were born, my husband and I had a relaxing, quiet evening playing Scrabble. About midnight, he went to check on the babies and called out to me. I knew before going upstairs that one of them was dead. I just knew.

We called 911 and rushed Vanessa to the hospital. It was no use; they could not revive her. We were devastated! Hours later, we were driving home when the most bizarre thought came into my head, "I hope Carolyn doesn't mind sharing her body." I just let that thought go. It seemed like such a weird thing to think in the midst of this tragedy. Of course, I didn't share this crazy thought with anyone. I wondered where that idea came from!

Then something very strange started happening. We could always tell the twins apart because Vanessa often had a look we called "the grumpy face." Carolyn had her own unique expressions, but we had never seen her with that look. The next day, Carolyn started making the exact grumpy face her twin used to have. My husband and I both saw it as plain as day. When Carolyn made the grumpy face I remembered that crazy thought about Carolyn sharing her body with Vanessa. I guess it wasn't so crazy after all.

I took Carolyn's grumpy face as a sign that Vanessa was around in Spirit and able to inspire Carolyn to communicate that idea to us. As I realized this, another strange thought came into my head, "I still have all my children with me—just a little less flesh."

I had the comfort of these spiritual experiences and yet my grief was still intense. I know it would have been worse without all the signs I was given. I got up every morning and had to function because there were three living children who needed me. They were all under three years old and too young to understand what was happening. They just kept singing and laughing; they could make me smile even when I thought I would never be fully happy again. So I would laugh with my little ones between the waves of grief that washed over me. Thank God for those moments of joy. I had a reason to go on living.

A friend introduced me to Reiki, a form of energy healing, and I knew right away that this was the healing method for me. I became an avid practitioner and my children loved receiving Reiki energy—it always seemed to calm them down. Carolyn was six years old and I was giving her a session when I heard a voice say, "Tell Carolyn I walk with her at school."

I often get impressions of the spirit world when I do healing work, and within a few minutes I knew without a doubt this was Carolyn's twin sister talking to me; yet I resisted delivering the message. Then, Vanessa said it again and again, getting more insistent each time.

Finally, I hesitantly said, "Vanessa is here and she wants me to tell you that she walks with you at school."

Carolyn responded, "Oh, I know. I feel her hand in mine."

She didn't even sound surprised—just very matter of fact—like it was as plain as breakfast.

This experience with my daughters showed me that Vanessa and Carolyn are still very connected. I now know that my twins walk hand-in-hand and are bonded heart-to-heart. My own heart is filled with peace when I think of them together in this unique way—one has a body and the other is pure spirit.

Spirit Babies With Family Ancestors in Heaven

When an infant crosses over, it is very comforting for parents and other loved ones to know that family ancestors are with the spirit of their beloved baby on the other side. The following stories illustrate the eternal soul love among family members in heaven.

Heidi and Great-Grandma Janet:
Into My Mother's Waiting Arms

Heidi was a sweet-natured baby who was born with numerous internal problems and a badly deformed foot. By some miracle, this little infant stayed alive in the neonatal unit for six months. Finally, the doctors gave up hope of her ever being able to live without life support.

When it was time to take Heidi off the machines, the family gathered at her bedside to send her Home with love. Heidi's great-grandmother, Rev. Janet, went down the hall to seek some solitude and pray for Heidi, as well as the whole family. As she prayed for strength, Janet was given a healing vision.

I saw my mother as a spirit; she had passed over the previous year at the age of ninety-nine. She had this joyous smile and was surrounded with angelic hosts. There was this huge gathering of angels and spirits of other family members who had gone before mother.

Mother put her hands out and said, "Come! Come!"

Then I saw my precious great-grandbaby run into my mother's waiting arms. Her foot was perfect! Heidi had no trouble running in the spirit world!

My heart was filled with love and gratitude as I walked down the hospital corridor and entered Heidi's room. I picked up Heidi and said, "Jesus is coming. He loves you so much."

Heidi opened her eyes and smiled. Then I heard these words, "I love you. See you later."

Heidi made her transition minutes later when the machines were disconnected. My mother and Heidi were so joyous in my glimpse of their world that I simply had no grief. This healing vision was a time of re-awakening to the joy of Spirit! Indeed, my heart was filled with joy instead of pain.

Miranda and Grandma Joyce: A Heavenly Circle of Love

Joyce arrived at my office with the intention of alleviating the grief of her mother's transition. It had been a difficult five years. Her grief was compounded because she had first lost her infant granddaughter Miranda, then her father, and now her mother.

After my mother's transition, I was doing some healing sessions to soothe my aching heart. One day, Dr. Wesch and I were visualizing divine love filling my heart when everything opened up. Then I was given this little glimpse of heaven.

I saw a little girl with long, brown hair dressed in a Holly Hobby dress. It was a long, old-fashioned dress like the young girls wore in "Little House on the Prairie." I knew without question that it was my granddaughter Miranda! I was thrilled because she looked so happy.

Next, I was given a vision of this group of people holding hands in a big circle. Both my mother and father were in the circle, and their faces were very clear; strangely, I couldn't recognize anyone else because their faces were faded. Somehow, I knew it was a gathering of all our relatives who had gone before Miranda.

The circle was filled with good feelings—like everyone was very safe and protected. I got the idea that everyone cared for each other and there was a lot of love. Actually, the words that came to me were "a circle of love." Soon after the vision started, I saw Miranda run into my mother's arms, and my mom embraced her. What a glorious sight!

Tears of joy streamed down my face, and my heart felt lighter in an instant. It all happened so fast. My grief was lifted; then peace and joy filled my heart.

Whenever I find myself missing Mom, Dad, or Miranda, I remember this vision and imagine them over there together in the circle of love. Then, once again, peace fills my heart.

Rachel and Julie: Friends Are Family Too

Julie is very sensitive and has had psychic gifts her whole life. As a child, she had an imaginary friend named Janie who came to play with her whenever she was alone. Intuitive abilities seem to run in the family; Julie remembers her aunts talking about deceased loved ones appearing in their living room. Julie reported rather nonchalantly, "My aunts seemed to think this was just an ordinary happening."

Julie was filled with grief when she miscarried early in her first pregnancy. On occasion, Julie receives a message from the spirit of her miscarried baby, who comes to her as a little girl. One day she heard this familiar little girl's voice saying, "I love you, Mommy. I want you to call me Rachel." It was an awesome moment for this grieving mother. Obviously, Julie and Rachel have a very strong love bond though Julie is still on earth and Rachel is in the spirit world.

Two years after the miscarriage, Julie attended an evening of meditation with Sylvia Browne, the famous psychic who frequently appeared on *The Montel Williams Show*. There was a very large audience in the auditorium, and Sylvia led a group meditation. Julie wanted to know if her baby was okay, so she set her intention to connect with Rachel's spirit. Julie described what happened that night.

Sylvia directed us to go to a comforting, quiet place. I remember this experience like a very vivid dream. My spirit left my body and soared above the meditation group—I found myself in another place with lots of people. Grace Jones, a wonderful healer friend who died several years earlier, appeared in this group of people. My heart flew open because I was so glad to see her again.

Suddenly, I noticed my baby was sitting on Grace's lap. Rachel looked to be about two years old with light brown wavy hair. She was barefoot and wearing a simple white dress. She had this real sweet energy about her. There she was—all curled up in Grace's lap. My dear friend was taking care of her!

I was so happy to see that my baby's spirit was with this special being. This experience was very precious and very powerful. I was filled with great joy.

Julie was named after her aunt, who was also a very powerful intuitive. Several years after the miscarriage, Aunt Julie reported, "Rachel is growing up on the other side. I see her often in my meditations and most of the time she has no shoes."

This report was comforting to Julie because it confirmed her own visions of Rachel growing older in heaven. Julie's beloved aunt died three years after the miscarriage, and Julie had this dream three weeks later:

In my dream, my aunt Julie appeared with her sister, Rose. My aunt Rose had a great sense of humor and was always being silly, so it seemed very natural when she appeared with this really big smile.

My two aunts were sitting together with my little girl between them. All three were glowing. There were no words—just the vision of the three of them together.

I am so very grateful that Rachel is surrounded, cared for, and loved by so many people who have heart connections with me.

These visions of Rachel in heaven brought much comfort to this grieving mother, and remembering them always brings joy to her heart. About once a year, Julie receives a delightful gift: she awakens in the morning, remembering a dream where she hears Rachel's voice saying, "Mommy, I love you."

Starlet and Sylvia: A Family Portrait

Sylvia felt very comforted when she received a vision of Starlet, her spirit baby, on the other side surrounded by loving family members. This vision is a much-treasured gift.

I lost my grandmother Tutu just a few months before Starlet was born. Tutu means "grandma" in Hawaiian. She was my dad's mom and I was always very close to her. We were always able to share everything, and I missed her being here to love and admire my baby. After Star made her transition, I believed in my heart that she was with Tutu.

This was confirmed when I received a vision of my two grandmothers and my daughter together in heaven with my Uncle D.J.—everyone looked so happy. I was in a dreamy state of mind but I wasn't asleep—it was more like a daydream. It seemed strange, because they were dressed as if they were here on earth. Tutu was holding Star, and the way they stood there reminded me of how people pose to take a family portrait. This vision lasted probably only five to ten seconds, but it seemed like a lifetime. It made me feel good just knowing all these people I love so dearly are together in heaven. I had a feeling of bliss!

Star also stays connected to my family here on earth. My dad has days when he can't stop thinking about her. He always calls to tell me when this happens, and we'll spend time talking about Star. This same thing happens with my mom.

It seems they always call when I need it the most! When I'm down or when I have one of my blah days—it's then I get a call because someone has been thinking of Star and me. I believe she is communicating through them to say, "I'm still here." After I hear she has been with my mom or dad, I get a warm glow, like "Star-light" inside of me. I feel uplifted and know that Star is watching out for her mom!

Isn't it great how she ties us all together again and again with memories of her? Star is a source of comfort for me and everyone else in the family. Her memory lives on through these other family members.

Charles and Deborah: We Are With Each Other

Deborah shared this fascinating story about her younger brother, who died as an infant when she was two years old.

My baby brother Charles, who was born with a hole in his heart, lived only two months and my parents never spoke of him again. There were no pictures of him displayed in our house. It was a closed subject in our family; in fact, in my younger years, I didn't even know he existed.

When I was ten years old, my mother decided to tell me about this deceased baby. Finally, I understood why I had a recurring dream of a baby dying. This dream went on for years, but once I knew the truth, the dream stopped. It seems some part of me knew the truth all along and was trying to bring it to my attention. Of course, it never occurred to me to tell anyone about my dream. Sadly, I suffered in silence all those years.

My early thirties was a very difficult time for me; first my grand-mother died and then, a few years later, my father. I was in deep grief because I was very close to both of them. Weeks after my father's death, my deceased grandmother and my baby brother appeared to-gether one afternoon while I was lying on my bed meditating.

Surprisingly, my brother appeared as an adult. Even though he was all grown up, there was no mistaking this spirit was my brother. He looked like a combination of me and my other brother, who is still living. I was so surprised because he was an infant when he died. Grandma appeared looking just like she did when she passed at age seventy-seven.

Both Grandma and Charles looked very happy, and together they sent me this message: "Your father is okay. It's time for you to take care of yourself now. Don't cry for us. We are with each other and we are okay."

It was so very comforting to see them together. To this day, I know they are here for me—like they're watching over me.

Spirit Babies Assist Family Members on Earth

After transition, spirit babies vibrate at a very high frequency and send powerful medicine to their loved ones and family on earth. Like angels, they work behind the scenes guiding, teaching, inspiring, uplifting, and healing the hearts of those they love. Their influence is so subtle and comes on the wings of such pure love that recipients often receive the benefit with no conscious awareness of the healing that has taken place. As Wachan, the Inca medicine man, said, *"The babies are the keepers of purity—they bring us light."*

These next stories illustrate some of the ways spirit babies bring light, love and healing to their family members.

Judith and Rosalyn: We Were Integrated Like Twins

Rosalyn is a born psychic. She is now in her sixties and has had a very rewarding career using her psychic gifts to help others receive messages from loved ones on the other side. Rosalyn's natural psychic abilities allowed her to have a memorable mystical experience when she was merely three years old. This is the story as told to me by Rosalyn.

Judith, my baby sister, died a few weeks before her first birthday. While sitting at her funeral, I suddenly saw her floating off to my right side. She was just sticking near me and watching. This took place sixty years ago, but I remember her floating there like it was yesterday. I was only three years old, so I didn't know this wasn't supposed to happen.

The spirit of my baby sister came home with me and stayed a very long time. In the early years, I could see her and hear her voice just as if she still had a body. Gradually, this faded, but I knew she was around because important ideas would come filtering into my mind. You might say she inspired me the rest of my life.

Judith would have been a great psychic if she had lived. She is one of my spirit guides and helpers; her main purpose is to help me develop my psychic abilities. We live in different dimensions (earth and heaven) but we work together with great ease. We are integrated like twins.

Judith has taught me that both time and space are really of no consequence. There are no barriers between the dimensions—unless you believe there are. My barrier is very thin—thanks to Judith.

I've had great assistance in developing my psychic gifts. While my grandmother was here in the physical world, she taught me how to connect with spirit beings. Then, I found I had a guardian angel who appears and assists me in giving people spiritual wisdom. I also have the spirits of my grandmother and Judith, my infant sister, helping me from across the veil.

I am very blessed. I never feel alone, and I always trust that all my spirit helpers will guide me as I work to connect human beings with the spirit world.

Here we see two souls working together for their mutual benefit. Judith, the baby who transitioned to the spirit world, fulfills her purpose of being a teacher and guide to her sister Rosalyn on earth. At the same time, Rosalyn does her own soul work as a spiritual teacher for people who come seeking guidance. Rosalyn and Judith work in tandem, evolving together as they help others advance to higher levels of consciousness.

Peter and Tracy: Hidden Moon Connection

Tracy, Peter's mother, shared this fascinating story about discovering that her spirit son had an important connection to the moon. These are her words.

Peter, our first child, was stillborn five days after his due date. By my calculations, Peter was due on a full moon, and that night, my husband and I decided to watch Moonstruck. *Four nights later, still waiting for the blessed event, we went to a local theatre just to pass the time. After looking at six different options, we decided to see* Apollo 13, *the story of three astronauts who went to the moon. It was another unconscious choice involving the moon.*

Peter was moving a lot while I sat watching this movie. Though I didn't know it at the time, he probably did his "final flurry" during one of the loud scenes in the movie. I went into labor the next day, but Peter never came home.

During the pregnancy, we collected a few picture books to prepare for our first baby's arrival. One of our favorites was Guess How Much I Love You *by Sam McBratney. At the very end of the story the father rabbit tells his little bunny, "I love you to the moon and back."*

After Peter died, we wrote him a letter on the inside cover of this book. We placed the book in the casket along with some other special things. In retrospect, it is uncanny that we chose that book. Now it looks like we must have known about Peter and the moon connections; but, at the time, we really had no clue.

Two years after losing Peter, our family was blessed with a healthy baby girl. Prior to our daughter's birth, we agreed on the name Cilene. My husband, however, preferred it as Selene.

Shortly after her birth, my husband's colleague, an English teacher, sent us a photocopy from a book of Greek mythology. Selene was known as "the goddess of the moon!" To this day, I get shivers all over my body whenever I think about it.

Funny, Selene also seems to have a moon connection. We both love to be outdoors, so when Selene was an infant, I often took her outside. I would wrap her in a blanket so we could watch the moon rise. She was fascinated—even saying "moo-moo" when she found the moon in the night sky.

I always thought of Peter when Selene and I were together watching the moon. I believe he's her guardian angel, and I always call on him to protect our beautiful little moon goddess.

Peter certainly is our little moonchild! Right from the beginning, we had a moon connection with him. Each individual moon connection didn't mean much when it was happening; in fact, we missed the significance completely. The birth of our daughter Selene was the catalyst for opening our eyes to the synchronistic happenings involving Peter and the moon. It was three years after Peter's death when all the pieces of the puzzle finally fell into place! It turned out to be a fascinating story once we discovered all the connections.

This powerful spirit baby is acting as a guardian angel for his younger sister. Peter presents himself as an influential communicator, and his parents are open to receiving his subtle symbolic messages. He gave enough clues for his family to connect the dots so they could awaken to the bond between the siblings—brother in heaven and sister on earth.

Riley and Aunt Ann: Connected to Family Forever

Ann shared this dramatic story of communication and healing from the spirit of her beloved niece, Riley Ann.

We are a big Irish Catholic family—my parents, siblings, and all the cousins are very connected. We were all terribly grief-stricken when my sister Maureen's first baby, Riley Ann, lived only two weeks. Our little Riley Ann was the catalyst for my spiritual awakening—she's what I call my "Oh, My God!" connection. She became my teacher and guide for my journey through grief.

Maureen and I both believed Riley had the power to send some kind of message from the other side, and we hoped for a sign or a dream. Nothing came. After several months, Dorothy, a friend of the family, called to report a dream about Riley.

> *I was in church and this little girl came walking up the aisle bouncing a ball. She looked to be about three years old, and she kept bouncing the ball and trying to get my attention. I didn't want to gawk in church, so I didn't turn around to look at her. Finally, she walked up the rest of the aisle to the pulpit, looked right at me, and said, "Do I have your attention?" Indeed, my attention was riveted on this insistent little girl.*
>
> *From the pulpit she asked, "Do you know who I am?"*
>
> *I answered, "No, I don't."*
>
> *Then she announced, clear as a bell, "I am Riley Ann. Please tell my mom I'm in a very good place. Everything is okay here. I'm very happy. Tell her not to worry."*

We were all overjoyed with this sweet message of comfort and love from Riley Ann. My sister Maureen, however, had such mixed feelings. She was very relieved and elated to know her spirit baby was happy. At the same time, she was sad and a bit hurt that her spirit daughter didn't come to her directly. She said at the time, "I know Riley Ann didn't come to me because I'm so grief-stricken." I thought the same thing. It just seemed right.

Five Years Later

We didn't hear anything more from Riley Ann for a very long time. Five years later my mother was in hospice care at a nursing home. She could not communicate because early-onset Alzheimer's had taken her voice a number of years before. Nevertheless, we could tell she was fighting to stay here with us. We stayed by her bedside around the clock, praying she would come to peace before making the journey Home.

Dad followed an old Irish tradition of lighting three candles to represent the trinity—Father, Son, and Holy Spirit. He placed the candles on the windowsill, believing these would help light the way for his beloved wife. He left the curtains open so the spring air could cool off my mother, who was very warm as she struggled to stay here on earth.

Dad and I sat holding vigil by the candlelight, but at about three in the morning, I left my mother's bedside briefly to get some fresh water for Dad and me. When I returned, the curtains were closed, and my father announced with great concern, "There's someone out there. I heard someone outside bouncing a ball on the sidewalk and then throwing it against the screen." He seemed quite freaked out, and I'm sure he was afraid somebody was out there to do harm.

I knew immediately that it was Riley Ann bouncing her ball to let us know she was here to take her grandma Home. I was thrilled to know she had come! I considered it such a blessing that she was joining the family for this vigil. In the moment, I simply assured Dad that everything was okay.

Later, as we continued the vigil over Mom, I told Dad that I knew the "someone out there" was our Riley Ann. His face softened, and his eyes filled with tears as I told him about Riley bouncing the ball up the church aisle in Dorothy's dream. For whatever reason, we hadn't told him this story before. My father is a man of prayer and great religious faith, and the thought of his granddaughter being present brought him so much peace. He had no trouble believing she had come to help.

Mom died at seven the following morning, just hours after Riley announced her presence with the sound of a bouncing ball. Dad and I both believe Riley came to help her grandma walk the bridge to the other side, but it's not something Dad ever discusses with anyone but me. It was a blessed gift for us to witness this act of love, and we consider it a sacred memory we share privately.

My heart was filled with grief at losing my mother, but this precious visit from Riley brought a spark of joy in the midst of the sadness. I was filled with gratitude that she came with a sign that I could recognize. It's amazing to me she could make her presence known. I no longer think of her as a baby or a little girl. Riley Ann was a healer for the whole family that night. She's a very powerful spirit!

Riley Assists Again

Nine months later our family pulled together once again to hold a bedside prayer vigil. Riley's mother, my sister Maureen, was at my home preparing to make her transition after surrendering to a very aggressive form of cancer. As a family we were in shock and deep grief to be repeating this scene. My father and I said the rosary over and over together as we waited for another passing. Sometimes we took turns sleeping. One night, not long after midnight, my sister reported a waking dream.

> *All these people are here to welcome me Home. They are all here waiting for me with open arms. There are so many of them! I can't see their faces yet, but I know I will.*

> *It feels so good to be in their love. Mom is here. She's not sick anymore. I'm so ready to go. I'm so anxious to go be with Riley Ann again. She's waiting for me.*

My whole being was filled with awe as I shared this holy moment with my dying sister. It's a sacred memory that will stay in my heart forever.

Several nights later, I was alone by Maureen's bedside praying for a peaceful transition and waiting for a sign from Riley that she had come to take her mom home. The candlelight made a faint glow in the room and you could hear a pin drop in the silence.

Suddenly, I heard the sound of multiple balls hitting the roof all at one time. It was so loud it sounded like somebody was throwing bowling balls on the roof. The whole house shook, yet no one else was awakened by the commotion. This was a sign from Riley meant just for me. She knew that balls being thrown was the one way I would recognize her presence. Yes, like she had for her grandma ten months earlier, Riley Ann had now come to escort her mom to her new life in heaven.

In the moment, I took great solace knowing Riley Ann was guiding her mother to the other side. It made me feel better somehow to know my dear sister was resting in the loving arms of her powerful spirit baby and our dear mother.

Another Healing Dream

Just a week after my sister died, Riley came to my teenage son in another powerful healing dream. His eyes filled with awe and wonder as he told me the dream.

> *I saw Aunt Moe Moe being lifted up to heaven. There were thousands and thousands of angels gathered around, singing. The gates of heaven opened and she walked through the gates. Grandma and Riley Ann both welcomed her with open arms on the other side. Riley looked to be about three years old. It's so wonderful to see them healthy and not sick anymore. They are just so happy to be together again. They seemed to be celebrating. It was awesome!*

Once again, Riley Ann came to help the whole family heal from our grief. She is a very powerful healer indeed! We are so blessed she stays connected and wants to help us heal.

Riley Visits Her Dad

After Maureen's passing, her husband, Doug, was left to parent their three young boys, who were all involved in sports activities. My sister always kept the house and the downstairs family room clean and picked up. In spite of his grief, Doug was trying to do the same. Each time he and the boys left the house, he made it a point to clear the floor in the family room by stacking all their sports gear in one corner of the room. Shortly after my sister's death, Doug noticed something very strange. He told me this story.

> *We left the house and came back, and it felt like someone had been there in the family room. Strangely, I found my big Pilates ball in the center of the room. And I absolutely knew the kids and I had picked up everything and put that ball in the corner with all the other gear. There's no way it could have rolled out by itself. I believe it was a sign from Riley Ann and her mom. It's really comforting to know they were here watching over us.*

To this day, it touches me deeply to know Riley Ann came to help her father heal his broken heart. She is such a powerful spirit!

Riley and John Edward

Seven years after Riley Ann passed, I had the opportunity to be in the gallery for a taping of John Edward's television show, Crossing

Over. *Of course, I was hoping and praying this famous medium would deliver a message from one of my family members. My prayers were answered when John focused on me and said:*

> *Your mother, your sister, and her baby are all together. They want me to tell you they will forever be your family even though they are on the other side. I'm also getting the impression you've lost two babies. They are here, and they want you to know they are safe and loved with your mom, your sister and her baby.*

I knew about one miscarriage, but I was not aware I had lost two beautiful souls. And while I was sad to hear this, I took solace that these two babies who never made it here are with their grandma, aunt Moe Moe, and cousin Riley. What three more beautiful souls could I have watching out for them until I meet them again? The bonds we have with our loved ones really are everlasting!

Riley continues to guide me on this fascinating spiritual journey. I've learned so much about the spirit world from her. Most importantly, I've learned our whole family is still connected on the other side, and death does not sever those bonds—or that love.

♥   ♥   ♥

Summary of Chapter Five

1) Young children are more open than adults to sensing spirits. They have not been conditioned to doubt or resist the supernatural, so spirit communication is natural to them. It is quite common for children to see the spirits of deceased infants and have conversations with them.

2) Children usually accept spirit relationships as normal; in fact, they frequently have spirit playmates who are visible to them but invisible to adults.

3) Spirit babies are not helpless like babies in the physical world. Indeed, they are powerful beings who share spiritual wisdom, inspire and assist family members, and send powerful medicine to loved ones on earth. A spirit baby can even act as a guide to help others accomplish their soul work.

4) Spirit ancestors assist babies as they make their transition to the other side. This is true even when the two have never met in the physical world.

5) Spirit babies always know how to find and recognize family and loved ones on earth as well as in heaven. Everyone stays connected through eternal bonds of love.

6) Many times the connection between siblings on opposite sides of the veil is very strong; yet, it is not at all obvious. It usually takes some intuitive awareness to discover that the siblings are still connected.

7) Love bonds go beyond genetics. In the spirit world there is no separation and everyone is considered family—our earthly distinctions of stepfamilies and in-laws are not recognized. These love bonds extend even to dearly loved family friends.

8) Infants who have transitioned often show themselves to loved ones as a spirit baby because that's how family members will most easily recognize them.

9) Spirit babies grow up on the other side. Even though they died as an infant, they might present themselves later to family members as older children or even adults.

10) A spirit baby sometimes communicates with numerous family members. As they share their stories and memories with each other, the fabric of the family is woven tighter and stronger.

Part II
You Can Heal Your Grief

This section offers an easy-to-follow map for healing grief after the loss of an infant. This map includes proven self-healing tools that are simple to learn and easy to use. Using these practical techniques will speed up your healing journey. In these five chapters you'll find true stories showing that it is possible for grieving family members to completely free themselves from suffering and transform their grief into joy.

CHAPTER SIX

~~~

Grief: Lost in the Darkness

*Grief forces you to look at those parts of yourself
that are not yet healed.
If you can look at grief as a teaching,
you will grow. The pain of grief is not the only
teacher in this life, but if looked at properly,
with awareness and an open heart,
it is one of the greatest teachers of all.*
—*Author Unknown*

In the first months after the loss of an infant, your heart demands all your attention. This is exactly as it should be. When your baby transitions from this earthly life, you naturally experience intense feelings, feelings as unique as you are. Your aching heart calls to be healed—yet you may have no idea how to begin.

Broken Heart—Shattered Life

If you are reading this book, you or someone you know has probably experienced the death of a beloved infant. A dearly loved baby has gone Home, but you are still here in this world with all your despair, loneliness, fear, anger, and perhaps guilt and shame. It's not unusual to feel like you are swimming in a sea of pain, awash with heartache. Your arms may ache to hold and kiss and cuddle your beloved baby. You may feel barren, empty, your heart crying out for what was to be. You probably created hopes and dreams for your little one that are now shattered, and your family is forever changed as a result. Indeed, your world is altered, and you may feel like nothing will ever be "normal" again.

It's common to feel alone in this deep grief and to pull your energy inward to protect yourself from the intense pain, to defend your hurt and vulnerable heart. While it's true that you are alone in your unique circumstance, you also share a common experience with other grieving parents—you have lost a tiny being that, once conceived, was expected to grow old. You have joined a "club" no one wants to join, where the membership dues are emotional pain, anguish, sorrow and grief.

As a gesture of deep compassion, others who have experienced the emotional turmoil you feel right now have volunteered to share their stories. It is their wish to show you that you are not alone in your heartache, and that your thoughts and feelings are very normal. The pain is different for everyone, but in their words you may find an echo that gives voice to your own indescribable grief. As you read these stories, please remember that these people did indeed heal their terrible heartache.

Stephanie, Dillon's Mom

I'm in total disbelief. Babies don't die in this day and age. How can this be happening to me? My heart is permanently broken. Pain. Pain. Pain. I don't think I will ever heal from this pain. It's all-consuming. My world has ended and I just want to die to be with Dillon. Even my physical heart hurts. All I can do is cry. My husband is crying all the time, too. There's no stopping the tears. I have no control of anything.

Why? Why us? Why our little Dillon? Where is God? God can no longer help me. I keep asking "why" even though I know there's no answer. My heart is filled with anger, betrayal, bitterness, hopelessness, helplessness, sadness, jealousy, envy, resentment, self-pity, despair, loneliness, fear, grief and, at times, apathy.

Judith, Kate's Mom

The first six months after Kate's death were the darkest moments of my whole life. I absolutely wanted to die. I never really planned it out, but suicide became an obsessive thought. Even now, two years later, when life gets overwhelming, my thoughts go there almost automatically.

Darlene, Mother of the Twins

When I first delivered our twins prematurely, I was shocked. How could my babies die? I remember the first time I cried. I was in the shower after getting home from the hospital and just lost it because I no longer felt my pregnant stomach. I cried and cried from that point on.

I was deeply depressed for my whole maternity leave. I would sleep curled up with the blankets that were made for the twins. I wouldn't go anywhere, or even get showered and dressed for the day.

At that time, I just kept asking myself why. "Why? Why did this happen?" I also kept talking to the babies, asking them to come visit me so I could know they were in heaven and were okay in their spirit life.

Dan, Cole's Grandpa

I was at the hospital at two a.m. when the doctors told us our grandson, Cole, wasn't going to make it. I got an unbearable pain in my chest and broke into deep uncontrollable sobbing. The intense grief I felt actually brought me to my knees—and I wasn't even embarrassed.

There Is a Spiritual Solution to Your Human Pain

As mentioned previously, these grieving parents and grandparents did heal their devastating heartache, though it was not accomplished overnight. The process was different for everyone, and the amount of time it took varied. But in every case these grieving loved ones, like many others, found that opening to the spiritual aspect of their experience was the essential element that made healing a reality. They each found a way to clear their human pain, reach out for spiritual assistance, and fill their hearts with peace, joy, and love. The stories of how they brought Spirit into their lives will unfold as you continue to read. For now, I ask you to simply trust that there is a spiritual solution to your pain, even though at the moment you may not know how to find it.

A Forest of Grief

Imagine for a moment that your grief is a gigantic forest, and you are lost in the deepest part where the trees are so thick you can't even see the light of day. As you walk in the darkness you come across many paths. Each time you ask, Is this the way out? You have no answer, for you cannot see where any of these paths lead.

Now imagine that you are flying above the forest, where you can look down and see all the paths weaving back and forth through the dense vegetation. From this vantage point high above the trees, you can easily find the way out.

This little story has a great message. You need to "get above" the problem to find the solution, for you cannot solve a problem at the level at which it was created. Your grief was created at the human level, so you cannot heal it if you stay focused on your human experience. So what is above your humanness?

It's your *soul*! You are actually a spiritual being experiencing what it means to be human. You might say that your soul exists above your human personality, and just as it can lead you out of the dense, dark forest, it can also lead you out of your grief. Your soul has the ability to guide and inspire you; in fact, it does so all the time whether you are aware of it or not.

You may or may not be in touch with your soul, but you can open to a connection with this most important aspect of yourself, and then learn how to create a spiritual solution to your human problem of grief.

The "Why" Questions

If you're like many parents who have lost an infant, you may find yourself asking why. You probably wish to make sense of this seemingly senseless tragedy. The human need to comprehend the workings of the world and to see it as a logical place may lead you to ask, "Why me? Why my baby? Why, why, why?"

Your answers to the "why" questions will be determined by your spiritual beliefs, that is, your views about life, death, the afterlife, grief, suffering, and healing. Your beliefs about destiny, fate, and whether the universe is random or ordered will also influence your answers. These are all spiritual issues, and what you hold as true in these matters affects your thoughts, your feelings and your ability to heal.

Most people's beliefs are a combination of what's been handed down through their family traditions, what they took in from their religious training, and what they have learned from life experiences. Your loss may generate many profound questions about issues you've never had to think of before. Trust that these questions come from the still, small voice of your soul—that's why they keep cropping up. Your soul wants you to heal and find peace once again, so it inspires you to ponder the philosophical issues that will help you resolve your grief.

I invite you to take some time to explore the answers that spring from your own belief system, while keeping an open mind to new possibilities. After all, you have a very wise soul that will bring you insights as you look for ways to understand your experience of life, death, and the afterlife. Use the following list of questions to explore what you believe to be true. Most of the questions have many answers, and many of those may be true at the same time. Don't judge or censor yourself—just notice what comes to mind.

Life:

Does my life have a purpose?

Did my baby's life also have a purpose?

What am I supposed to learn from losing my baby?

Can I see a tragedy as an opportunity for growth?

Death:

What happens when we die?

Did my baby die at the wrong time?

Who is to blame? Me? The doctor? Fate? God? Who?

Is there a spiritual reason for my baby's death?

Afterlife:

My baby is dead. How is it possible that I sometimes feel my baby around me?

Does my baby have an eternal spirit?

What happened to the spirit of my baby?

Did my little one become an angel?

Will I see my baby again in heaven?

If my baby is on the other side, will he or she remain an infant forever?

Who is taking care of my baby now?

Grief:

Is it good to mourn? If so, for how long?

Is there such a thing as too much grief, or bad grief?

Will I ever get over this?

Can I die from this broken heart?

If I laugh or have fun, am I dishonoring the memory of my baby?

Suffering:

Is suffering a natural part of being human?

How long will I suffer?

What did I ever do to deserve this?

Does God want me to suffer?

Am I being punished?

Will any good come from all this suffering?

Does my suffering affect my baby in heaven?

Healing:

What's the difference between coping and healing?

Is it possible to truly heal after my baby is no longer on earth?

Can I find peace after the pain of a miscarriage?

Will I ever laugh again or feel the joy of life again?

Is it safe to love another baby?

Can I open my heart to love again?

The Nature of Spirit:

Does my baby know what I'm thinking?

Is my precious daughter aware I'm praying for her?

Does my son know I still feel great love for him?

Is it possible that my baby knows my heart is breaking?

What happens to the spirits of miscarried babies?

Is there such a thing as divine order or divine timing?

Am I just unlucky or was all this "meant to be?"

Different Answers for Everyone

The answers to these questions are different for everyone. You may even find that the answers that make sense to you now are different from the ones you'd have given a few years ago, or the ones you'll give tomorrow. As a soul you are here on earth to be an ever-changing, evolving human being. The truths you carry with you today can be transformed as you move forward in life and as your experiences expand.

The death of an infant is a life-changing event. I ask you to keep an open mind as you seek new answers and new ways to heal your heart from this tragedy. Everyone's experience is unique and everyone grieves differently. There is no one right way to believe—or to grieve—or to heal. In addition, there is no right time for grieving to be finished. You will create your own personal and special healing journey—yet you do not have to figure it all out by yourself. Know that when you ask God, the angels, and your very own wise soul for help, the answers will come.

♥   ♥   ♥

Summary of Chapter Six

1) After the death of a baby, your world is altered, and you may feel like nothing will ever be "normal" again.

2) At this time, it's common to feel alone in your deep grief and to pull your energy inward to protect yourself from the intense pain.

3) You are not alone in your heartache, and your thoughts and feelings are very normal.

4) Most people want to make sense of a seemingly senseless tragedy. The human need to comprehend the workings of the world and to see it as a logical place may lead you to ask, "Why me? Why my baby? Why, why, why?"

5) Your answers to the "why" questions are determined by your spiritual beliefs, that is, your views about life, death, the afterlife, grief, suffering, and healing.

6) You cannot solve a problem at the level at which it was created. Your grief was created at the personality level, so you must change your perspective to the soul level to solve your grief issues.

7) Opening to the spiritual aspect of the grief experience is the essential element that makes healing a reality.

8) Your soul wants you to heal and find peace once again, so it inspires you to ponder the philosophical issues that will help you resolve your grief.

9) You have a very wise soul that brings you insights as you look for ways to understand your experience of life, death, and the afterlife.

10) There is a spiritual solution to your pain, even though at the moment you may not know how to find it.

CHAPTER SEVEN

Human Eyes and Soul Eyes

The greatest tragedy in human life
is to live unaware of one's divine identity.
—Rev. William Harper Houff, Author

You are human and you are divine; you are both at the same time. You are first and foremost a soul—and your soul has chosen to have a human experience. At birth you lost the conscious connection with your divine self, but your soul did not cease to exist. It is only your awareness of the connection that is forgotten and needs to be reawakened. The goal during your earthly journey is to reconnect with your spiritual essence—your soul—and to integrate its light and love into your human life.

There are always two levels of experience happening simultaneously: the human level and the spiritual level. This is true whether you are aware of both or not. Every event in your life—even your grief—affects you at both levels. You can choose to look at every experience through human eyes or soul eyes or both. Birth, life, death, and relationships, indeed, everything changes depending on your perspective.

When you experience life solely at the human level, you see only the physical world and nothing beyond it. You see through eyes of fear and have many judgments about right or wrong, good or bad, and beautiful or ugly. When you meet someone and utilize this perspective, you see their personality and physical body, but not their soul light. Most people view the world from this perspective, seeing life through only their human eyes.

In contrast, when you experience life from the soul perspective, you see with your spiritual eyes and perceive with divine love. You do not judge what is good or bad, right or wrong, beautiful or ugly. When you greet someone, you see first their divine essence and then become aware of the physical body and personality. When you use soul vision, you see love everywhere you look. Mother Teresa saw beauty in what most see as extreme ugliness because she viewed the world through eyes of love, through soul eyes.

Most people see the loss of an infant with their human eyes. Some are also able to see it with soul eyes. Learning about soul eyes gives you a choice about the way you experience the death of your baby. It is much easier to heal your grief and come to peace when you learn to see the loss of your infant through both human and soul eyes—at the same time. The following stories will help you develop soul vision and view the loss of your infant from this integrated perspective, just as these grieving parents did.

Seeing With Human Eyes Only

When people see the death of an infant with human eyes only, their focus is on the loss of the little baby body, and their infinite heartache seems unsolvable. From this perspective, everything dies with the death of the body, and it is very difficult to find any uplifting thoughts. They may have a philosophical idea that their baby has a spirit, but they don't know any practical steps they can take to relieve their grief.

Jenny and Colette: A Mother's Unresolved Grief

My heart went out to Colette the minute I saw her. She looked forlorn, lost, worn out; it was clear that she cared little about her appearance. I wondered what tragedy had caused her to lose so much of her natural radiance. Colette was quite overweight and seemed to be in her early forties. As our initial interview unfolded, I was shocked to discover she was only twenty-eight years old!

I soon learned the reason for Colette's loss of vitality; five years earlier, her beautiful baby girl was stillborn. She named her Jenny. Colette never recovered after this much-anticipated first pregnancy ended in tragedy, and she felt great despair that she had not conceived again. Despite her constant heartache, Colette did not even think to reach out to friends, grief support groups, or to seek professional help. She believed she should be able to handle her grief all by herself. Finally, when she found herself contemplating suicide, she decided to seek assistance.

Colette had all the classic symptoms of clinical depression: inability to sleep, joylessness, no interest in life, lack of motivation, absence of creativity, severe weight gain, and ongoing suicidal thoughts. She knew her grief about her baby's death was causing these problems; however, she had no clue about how to overcome her depression. Colette believed that the only solution to her grief was to have another baby, and she was greatly distressed that this was not happening.

Colette, like many grief-stricken loved ones, was unaware that she had a choice to see the loss of her infant through soul eyes. My hope for her healing journey was that I could teach her to release her pain and then help her shift her focus to a spiritual perspective.

Seeing With Soul Eyes Only

Some people see the loss of an infant with soul eyes only. They focus on ideas about eternal life and ignore their normal human feelings after a loss. This can interfere with the healing process just as much as using human eyes exclusively.

Amy and Rebecca: I Have No Grief

Amy was delivered stillborn with the umbilical cord wrapped around her neck. Amy's mother, Rebecca, was spiritually awake and was accustomed to using spiritual principles to guide her life. These are Rebecca's words just months after Amy made her transition.

> *I know my baby is in a better place. I don't need to grieve because I believe so strongly that all is in divine order. Her spirit is with God now and that's what was meant to be. I don't know why God took our baby, but I guess I don't have to know why. Everything happens for a reason even if we don't know that reason. I just keep imagining little Amy up there in heaven, so I have no pain to speak of. Whenever I start to cry, I just focus on the vision of Amy as an angel and I can calm myself. We plan to have other children, so I keep my thoughts directed on that dream and think about the future with them.*

Rebecca is seeing Amy's death only with soul eyes. She is also using spiritual principles to deny her natural, human emotions and bypass the need to feel and express her heartache. I use the phrase "spiritual bypassing" to describe this phenomenon. Spiritual bypassing may work for a while, but eventually Rebecca's suppressed emotions will cause emotional or physical problems unless she finds a way to address them.

Spiritual beliefs like Rebecca's are very helpful and uplifting. However, Rebecca skipped the crucial steps of feeling her emotions and then releasing them. At the moment, her grief is still present but hidden underneath her spiritual platitudes.

At some point in her healing journey, Rebecca needs to view her loss with human eyes, connect with her human pain, and release the heartache of losing her blessed little baby girl. Only then will she find true inner peace.

Seeing With Both Human Eyes and Soul Eyes

It is the soul of your baby that lights up your human heart, not his or her physical body. *It is the soul-to-soul connection with him or her that ignites the love you feel in your heart.* This might be a whole new way to look at the love you feel for your baby. We live in a society that emphasizes the physical aspects of life as opposed to the spiritual aspects, so we are programmed to focus on the physical. Consequently, people assume it is the physical body of a newborn baby that is creating the feeling of love in their hearts.

The pain you feel at the loss of your baby springs from your separation from his or her physical form *as well as* the loss of your heart connection. Both of these must be recognized and acknowledged as a legitimate part of your human experience—a loss viewed with human eyes.

When your soul eyes are open as well, you'll see that while your baby's body is gone, his or her spirit is not. At the soul level there is no separation, no loss of the connection you share with your beloved infant. You and your baby were family in eternity before incarnating, and you are still family even though his or her physical form is no longer with you. Your profound love arises from the connection between your souls that has always existed and will continue to exist forever.

Harrison and Sharon: Love in the NICU

Sharon's infant son Harrison lived only four months and never left the NICU. Sharon felt great heartache as she used her human eyes to watch her beloved infant struggle to live. But because she was spiritually aware, she was able to see a very different picture when she looked at Harrison with soul eyes. This courageous mother used these words to describe viewing her infant son from two very different perspectives—human eyes and souls eyes.

> *My heart broke when we got the news that our baby had serious medical problems and had almost no chance of surviving. The pain in my chest was so intense I thought I might have a heart attack. It was excruciating—like nothing I've ever experienced before or since. The worst was leaving my baby in the NICU when it was time for me to go home. I could hardly bear the pain of leaving him*

there. At home, I cried and cried until it seemed there could be no more tears. Sometimes it was what I call wailing and other times it was this deep sobbing. At times, there was only my pain—nothing else mattered.

Somehow I was able to rise above the pain and be the mother I wanted to be when I was with Harrison at the hospital. It was like I flipped a switch and replaced the pain with a deep spiritual love whenever I was with my baby. In his presence, I felt this soul love for Harrison and it lifted me to a different place.

In addition, I felt surrounded by God's love at the hospital. I could sense a spiritual light every time I entered the NICU. It was all around me even with all the machines beeping and people responding to codes. God and the angels were definitely present every minute of the day and night. For me, the NICU was a peaceful, comforting place to be, because I could feel the divine love energy there.

I could feel God working through the NICU doctors and nurses as they talked with the families and the babies. They are dedicated professionals who work with their hearts wide open, giving love along with the medical treatments. They took care of medical issues but they also focused on helping us all connect in love with our babies. They helped me bond with Harrison in numerous ways, but the "finger hugs" were the best. One day I sat next to Harrison's bed all day long as he wrapped his tiny little fingers around my index finger. Believe me, finger hugs became extremely special! I truly think the love does most of the healing.

Parents bonded with each other in the NICU as they shared heartaches and compassion. I could see people opening their hearts and forming this wonderful community of love. We even loved each other's infants! We celebrated each sign of improvement and supported each other during the down times. All lines of prejudice were automatically erased: race, color, religion and money made no difference in this unit where babies were fighting to live. This giving and receiving experience was like nothing I've ever seen before. All of us walked away totally changed.

In the midst of all this loving energy, I could stand beside a baby's little bed, look past all the tubes and machines, and see into the soul. It was soul touching soul in a place where time stands still. Each time it brought me back to the connection where we all started.

In his too-short time, Harrison was totally surrounded and wrapped in the loving embrace from God, his angels, his family, his caregivers, and the many folks who prayed for him and loved him from afar. I am so grateful he experienced so much love—he deserved every glorious morsel of it.

Sharon opened all her spiritual senses and saw beauty instead of the medical equipment, and therefore found peace amidst the chaos of the NICU environment. She spent day after day for four months in the NICU using her soul eyes to soothe her human pain. To become all we can be, we need only follow Sharon's example and live from an integrated perspective using our soul eyes and all our soul senses while we are in human form.

Harrison and Grandma Fran: Joy in the NICU

Fran is Sharon's mother and Harrison's grandmother. Fran, like her daughter, is spiritually awake and has the gift of being clairvoyant. Grandma Fran was also able to look at her beloved Harrison with both human eyes and soul eyes. These are her words.

Our whole family was devastated by the news about Harrison. My heart felt like it was seared with lightning and could never be healed. Within hours of hearing about my grandson, my whole body hurt from head to toe. It seemed like my emotional pain became physical pain and every cell was screaming. My fatigue was overwhelming—I could hardly get out of bed each day. Every morning when I opened my eyes, the grief hit me again as I groggily remembered the reality of Harrison fighting for his life in the NICU. I wanted to be there for my daughter and my grandson, yet I was having trouble coping myself. Like my daughter, I was uplifted by all the love surrounding our grandson in the NICU.

My grandson Harrison was a radiant baby—he absolutely glowed with love. His mission in life was all about love—he both generated love and attracted it. There was so much about this little baby that was extraordinary. He had an incredible presence and seemed to be a people magnet. All the hospital personnel became very attached to him, and everyone who came to the unit stopped by his bed to say hello. Many people came in who could sense a spiritual connection with Harrison, and they felt the love that was present. Most of them didn't have words to describe their experience, but they were always aware of the significance of this encounter. I see Harrison as a powerful healer—everyone who came into his presence was uplifted.

Harrison had numerous physical problems as well as Down's Syndrome, yet he was a content, peaceful baby. He retained an aura of love and joy regardless of all the problems. He did not seem to experience physical pain like we do, for he seldom cried—usually only when the monitors for the other babies went off. I could tell he still had a deep connection with the other side, and I think this allowed him to bear the pain of his condition.

We could rarely hold Harrison because of all the tubes. There were a few times when the staff allowed me to cuddle him next to my heart. Harrison just lay there and snuggled against me. I will always treasure those cuddles! It was like his little body was all heart. I could see sparkles of light shimmering all around us and feel the divine love. I could feel both his little human body and his divine soul at the same time. Time stood still in these magnificent moments.

We all learned so much from Harrison—most important was to focus on now. We learned to share love right now because we might not be able to do so in another hour. We learned to love life and treasure every moment. Harrison lived that way!

Sharon and Grandma Fran are both blessed with clairvoyant abilities, so they had glimpses of what was happening around Harrison in the spiritual realm. They felt uplifted and enriched when they used their soul eyes to see angels and divine light surrounding and protecting Harrison. Each day, Sharon and her mother moved back and forth between human vision and soul vision. They opened their hearts to falling in love with both his spirit and also his challenged little body.

These two women were grateful to have this additional spiritual perspective, as it provided a balance for the sorrow, anxiety, and helplessness they were feeling. They saw many others in the NICU who were not uplifted in this way and noticed that these stricken parents had no relief from their painful and fearful emotions. Most parents found it difficult to be in this intense atmosphere of the minute-by-minute struggle to live.

Our soul, our very nature, is divine love. It is the essential core of who we are. We each come to earth to become an expression of this love, to give voice and action to our true nature—and Harrison was no exception. Because they were able to see with both human eyes and soul eyes, Sharon and Fran were able to feel their human pain and then look past Harrison's physical challenges and see his true nature. They saw his greatness, his soul, and the divine love he embodied. In his four months here on earth, he was love, he radiated love, and he attracted love. The love he generated is still having a ripple effect that flows through his family and out into the world. It continues to grow even though he is no longer in body. Harrison came to teach about divine love—and he did, magnificently!

Family Members Often See With Different Eyes

We all have our own way of thinking about life and death. It is no surprise that members of the same family often have conflicting spiritual convictions about the death of an infant. These different spiritual viewpoints often cause disagreements that are difficult to resolve.

Thomas and Marcia: Your Own Saint in Heaven

Marcia lost her firstborn son, Thomas, just days after bringing him home from the hospital. She was filled with despair and could find no solace for her broken heart. Marcia told me this story illustrating that family members sometimes see with different eyes.

> *At Thomas' funeral, my mother-in-law greeted me with a big hug and said, "Congratulations! You now have your own saint in heaven." I was so angry she would say such an outrageous and hurtful thing to me when I was in such deep grief about losing my baby. I was in shock at the very idea! I didn't want to celebrate him being a saint in heaven; I wanted him here with me, where he belonged.*
>
> *Now I finally understand Thomas truly is my own saint in heaven and this gives me great comfort. It's taken me years to come to this understanding of the heart. Timing is everything.*

Thomas' grandmother had her own deep grief about losing Thomas. However, she was able to move back and forth between her human eyes and her soul eyes—and found comfort and reassurance in doing so—because some of her beliefs came from an old European culture. In the grandmother's tradition there was a strong belief that her grandson was now a special, heavenly connection for the family. These spiritual bonds were to be treasured and celebrated.

Marcia had no such beliefs to fall back on. As far as she could tell, there was no benefit to having her son in heaven. Marcia was immersed in despair, seeing the loss of Thomas exclusively with human eyes, while the grandmother proclaimed the joy she felt from seeing the situation with soul eyes. Sadly, these different points of view created a rift at a time when both women could have benefited from loving and supporting each other.

Each of us is able to see with soul eyes in our own time, in our own way—it cannot be forced. Marcia's journey of spiritual awakening came years later, when she was ready. Only then she was able to see her mother-in-law's point of view.

Annie and Richard: Two Opposing Viewpoints

Annie is a very practical woman, a scientist with a degree in medical technology, yet she has learned to see with soul eyes. She attributes her spiritual awakening to her mother's death.

My grief was devastating when my mother passed, and yet it opened me to an awareness of Spirit. Mom and I were so connected in life that we talked every day; we continued talking even after she went to the other side. Right after her transition, I talked to her in my head and actually heard her talking to me. We would carry on these conversations even while I was at work.

At first I didn't know if this was real, so I asked God for some kind of sign. An hour later I could smell her usual scent around me in the lab. To me this was a message saying, "This is real."

She's been gone ten years, and we still talk every day. Since her death, I can sense angels around me, and they send me guidance all the time. It's very comforting, and it puts everything in a different light.

Annie's strong heart connection and her deep desire to continue her relationship with her mother motivated her to become very adept at spirit communication. This skill became even more valuable as her life unfolded.

While her mother was still alive, Annie had three healthy children. After her mother's death, she delivered two stillborn boys, a year apart. In each case the baby's heartbeat stopped five months into the pregnancy—and in each case there was no medical explanation. Both times Annie had to go through labor and delivery knowing the baby was no longer alive. Her strong spiritual connection to her mother became her saving grace during this time and helped heal her grief.

Each time, I cried a lot when my husband and I held our son right after delivery. I also cried some through the funerals. Then I just kept thinking about my mother holding the baby in heaven, and my grief vanished. I can't think of anyone better suited to loving and caring for our sons than my mom.

Because I had so little grief, I kept wondering if there was something wrong with me. Did this mean I didn't love and want my babies? After much soul searching, I was able to answer with a resounding no. I trusted that the angels and my mom were uplifting me.

Richard, Annie's husband, had a very different reaction to the death of their babies. He cried all the time and went through a complete personality change. He could not seem to cope with the loss of his sons, and ended up in a long-term depression. Five years later he was still deep in despair. Sadly, he refused to accept any help. These are Annie's words about her husband.

Rich has become very bitter about life. He's angry all the time and has become verbally abusive, mostly toward the children. He cries and keeps talking about missing the babies. He is so absorbed in his grief that he is hurting the children who are still here. When I talk about the boys as spirits, he looks at me and says, "How can you think like that?"

Richard sees the death of the babies with only his human eyes. For him, death is the enemy. His soul eyes are closed, just as his mind is closed to his wife's beliefs about life after death. He doesn't understand why his wife has so little grief, and he is angry because his own grief is so great by comparison. Sadly, Richard chooses to keep his focus on his pain and recycle it over and over without releasing it. Consequently, he feels no relief and remains lost in despair, as though wandering through his own dark, lonely forest. Of course, he does not understand that his negative thoughts and feelings are holding him in this state of hopelessness. Only the bright light of Spirit can penetrate the darkness his human mind has created—but he must be open to the possibility. At this point in time, he is not.

Annie is able to see the death of their babies through both human and soul eyes. First, the human part of her released much heartache; she then chose to keep her focus on her divinity. Annie is able to live from both the soul and the human perspective, moving back and forth between the two. For her, there is no enemy called death because she knows the soul is eternal. In Annie's experience, the veil between the two worlds is very thin. She has embraced her new spiritual relationship with her sons and does not yearn to have them back in human form. Instead, she feels the joy of knowing they still exist in the spirit world.

Awakening to Soul Eyes

Most people are living their lives unaware of their spiritual nature and the otherworldly dimension that exists beyond our ordinary five-sense reality. They are busy with their everyday lives, focused on the material world while climbing the ladder of success. It is a very common way to live, and it usually works—until a crisis of some kind disturbs the flow of everyday life.

The death of a loved one is often the crisis that invites people to explore their spiritual nature and seek understanding about where we come from, why we are here, and where we go. Seeking a solution to grief often becomes the opportunity for spiritual awakening. During this sacred time of searching, you can begin to see the world with soul eyes, even if you have never done so before.

Sometimes It Just Takes Time

Grief and healing are different for everyone. It takes as long as it takes. Learning to see with soul eyes comes in different ways and at different times for each of us. Whenever it comes, healing is likely to shift to a whole new level.

For some people, the loss of an infant is simply too much to bear, and they are unable to do more than set their grief aside and cope. If you feel you are simply unable, just now, to see your experience through soul eyes, be gentle with yourself and give it time. I invite you to keep an open mind and continue reading; the information in this book will help you *when you're ready*. And if you're reading this many years after your loss, it may be that the time is right for you at last.

It is never too late to heal.

♥   ♥   ♥

Summary of Chapter Seven

1) You are human and divine; you are both at the same time.

2) You can see the loss of your baby through human eyes, through soul eyes, or through the integration of both perspectives.

3) Healing grief is most difficult if you see with human eyes only.

4) Viewing your loss with only soul eyes usually brings about spiritual bypassing—that is, using spiritual principles to justify denying normal, human grief.

5) Healing grief is easiest if you view your loss with both human eyes and soul eyes at the same time.

6) Seeking a solution to grief after the loss of a loved one often becomes an opportunity for spiritual awakening.

7) Spirit babies come as healers to grieving loved ones, just as the Inca spirit babies act as healers for the people of that ancient culture.

8) Family members sometimes have conflicts because they see the loss of an infant through different eyes and cannot understand the other's point of view.

9) Death is the enemy when you see the loss of your infant through human eyes only; however, there is no death when you see through soul eyes.

10) Learning to see with soul eyes shifts the healing process to a whole new level. It is never too late to open your soul eyes.

Chapter Eight

Healing Your Heart

Love is the most powerful healing force in the universe.
—Richard Gerber, M.D.

When you are filled with a powerful emotion like love or grief, it might not occur to you to step back to examine the essence of the emotion—what it's made of, or what physical sensations are associated with it. But with a little investigating, you will find that emotions are energy. This energy fills the cells of your body and even the energetic space around your body called your aura. Some emotions flow freely through your body, while others settle in like so much sludge. All of them generate a physical sensation in either a specific part of your body or throughout your whole system.

The energy of grief feels heavy, dark, crushing; it is usually felt in the chest, but it can also affect your whole being. The following descriptions of grief came from mothers, fathers and grandparents who were in the depths of despair after the death of a beloved infant.

- "My heart feels so heavy—there's a pressure inside my chest."
- "My whole body feels like lead. I'm moving in slow motion, including my brain."
- "There's a dark cloud around me all the time. It's even there when I wake up."
- "My shoulders feel weighed down like I'm carrying the weight of the world."
- "I feel like I'm moving under water most of the time."
- "I feel like I have an elephant sitting on my chest."
- "I've lost the lilt in my voice and the spring in my step."

In contrast, the feeling of love is light, luminous, and vibrant. It brings a sense of brightness to your whole being. The statements that follow are quotes from people who have used a simple imagery process to fill their whole system with the energy of spiritual love.

- ♥ "I feel like I'm glowing!"
- ♥ "When I look in the mirror, my eyes are sparkling."
- ♥ "I am absolutely radiant!"
- ♥ "I seem to be floating instead of walking."
- ♥ "I feel all lit up!"
- ♥ "I'm in love with life!"
- ♥ "I'm high on love!"

Think about what would happen if you could somehow open your heart, remove the grief energy that feels so heavy, and then fill your chest with the bright light of spiritual love. Just imagine the change that would take place. Chances are you would feel different both physically and emotionally. You would probably even look different. It sounds too good to be true, doesn't it? Well, as you will see, it is true—it is possible.

Radiant Heart Healing (RHH) is a model of spiritual healing that literally allows you to remove the energy of grief from your heart and replace it with the energy of love. It is a proven method that has worked repeatedly with many people in the throes of terrible grief, and the results are quite amazing. In a remarkable transformation, people release the heaviness in their hearts and start to feel lighter within minutes. Best of all, RHH is a process you can learn to do yourself.

Emotions, Energy, and Radiant Heart Healing

All of our emotions are composed of energy, and each feeling vibrates at its own specific frequency. Even if you have never thought about emotions in this way, you can intuitively feel a change as you shift through sadness, fear, anger, excitement, joy, and love. You may also sense a change as emotions shift in other people. The more sensitive you are, the more adept you will be at noticing the frequency changes in yourself, others, and the environment around you.

You have probably walked into a room and, without hearing any conversation, thought, "Oh, you can cut the tension in here with a knife!" In that moment you were sensing the low, heavy vibration of anger or frustration among those in the room. People sometimes refer to this intuitive process as "feeling the vibes." This slang expression really means "feeling the vibratory frequency of the energy."

At the other end of the spectrum, you may have felt the high vibrations of "love in the air" at a wedding, and your own heart was joy-filled as a result. Perhaps you have participated in a prayer circle where the high, fast vibration of divine love left you feeling lightheaded and lighthearted. The vibes at these events warmed your heart and uplifted your spirit.

Remembering any of these emotional experiences will remind you that you have already had many experiences of sensing the specific vibratory frequencies of various emotions. You can easily experience different vibes without ever knowing technical terms like "vibratory frequency of the energy of emotions."

David R. Hawkins, M.D., Ph.D. is an internationally recognized pioneer in the fields of consciousness research and spirituality. In his book *Power Versus Force: An Anatomy of Consciousness*, this licensed psychiatrist presents his pioneering work defining the vibratory frequency of various emotions. His research shows that guilt, shame, anger, fear, and grief have low, slow frequencies that actually weaken your energy field (aura) and leave you more vulnerable to physical and psychological illnesses. Hawkins also verifies that human love, joy, peace, and divine love have high, fast frequencies that strengthen your energy field, boost your immune system, and promote emotional well-being.

What does this scientific research have to do with healing your grief? You can heal your grief faster and more easily when you perceive it as energy and use energy techniques to remove it from your whole being. This is my conclusion after teaching hundreds of grieving people to use the RHH energy tools over the past thirty years.

Why is this so? *Radiant Heart Healing is designed to work with the energy of grief.* Grief, as an emotional energy, is very debilitating and can cause problems mentally, emotionally, physically and spiritually. Using RHH visualizations, you release the low, slow vibrations of the grief energy from the cells of your body, as well as from your aura. When this is completed, you visualize filling your body and your aura with the high, fast frequency of divine love. The RHH method is uniquely designed to return you to your natural state of radiance so you can live with renewed joy, passion, and zest!

Radiant Heart Healing

This model for healing grief consists of four components:

1) Releasing the energy of grief from your heart.
2) Filling your heart center with the energy of divine love.
3) Having an experience of meaningful spirit communication.
4) Shifting to a spiritual perspective about life here on earth and the afterlife.

Each of these components used independently will likely provide some relief to anyone who is grieving the loss of a loved one. Together, they create a comprehensive and integrated approach to healing after the loss of an infant.

The long-term goal of using the Radiant Heart Healing process is to remember your baby with love instead of pain.

I. Releasing the Energy of Grief From Your Heart

Both current grief and grief stored from years past create energy blocks in the body and the energy field that need to be cleared. Energy responds to visualizations (seeing pictures in your mind). You can use visualizations to remove grief energy from your body. Or, if you don't usually see pictures in your mind's eye, you can simply think about releasing heartache, and it will actually happen. The RHH release process facilitates this quickly and easily when you let go and flow with the process.

RHH Visualizations for Releasing Grief Energy

1) Find a quiet place to relax.
2) Invite your higher self, your spiritual guides, and the angels to assist in the release process.
3) Feel the grief you are holding and give it a color—any color but white.
4) Turn your attention to your physical body and carefully scan it to identify those areas where you are holding the grief energy (heart? head? hands? throat? knees? back? intestines? eyes?).
5) Give every cell permission to release the grief energy represented by the color you chose in #3.
6) Imagine each cell opening and little rivers of this same colored energy flowing though your body to form a ball in the center of your chest.

7) When this colored ball is full, visualize or think about releasing it as a geyser spraying out the front of your chest.

8) Ask your higher self, your spiritual guides, and the angels to help you; then continue to release until the geyser feels clear.

9) Again, scan your body to see if all the grief energy has been released. Be sure to check each area you identified in #4. If you find any color remaining, continue the visualization for a bit longer.

10) Spend a moment thanking your spiritual helpers. And thank yourself for being willing to let go of all this negative, life-draining energy.

During this process, most people feel a lessening of a weight or pressure in their chest. Those with soul vision may actually see a geyser of color flowing out in front of them. They might also see the energy gradually change colors until it fades to white or a very clear, transparent spray of energy. Others may not feel or see anything but will intuitively know when the grief energy is gone.

Releasing the energy of grief is an important step in achieving the long-term goal of remembering your baby with love rather than pain.

Crying—Another Way to Release

It is likely that you will find yourself crying as you do these RHH visualizations. This is often the case because crying is a natural way to release grief energy. I do not suggest you do this imagery work instead of crying. Doing the imagery work *and* crying at the same time is very powerful. Allow your tears to flow without restriction.

II. Filling Your Heart With Divine Love

This next RHH visualization is very important. You have created empty space in your heart center and in the cells of your body, so you need to fill them with energy again. After releasing the low, slow vibration of grief, you want to replace it with divine love. This energy is the highest possible frequency, and it comes directly from our Creator.

Love is the most powerful healing force in the universe. Divine love is the intense, bright light often reported by people who have survived a near-death experience. Some people feel this energy as heat or warmth moving through their body, while others see it as light; some people do both. Others get excellent results from just thinking about the love energy even if they don't feel it or see it.

RHH Visualization for Filling Your Heart With Divine Love

1) Imagine there is an open spot on the top of your head.

2) Now visualize a funnel that emerges from that spot and opens into the universe.

3) Next, scan the universe with your mind's eye and see a limitless ball of divine love. Visualize (or think about) this ball filled with divine love that looks like the sparkling, dancing light you see when the sun shines on the water.

4) Extend your funnel out into the universe to connect with this ball of love.

5) Draw the divine love and light into your funnel, down through the narrowing channel into the top of your head, and all the way down into your heart center.

6) Again, invite your higher self, your spiritual guides, and the angels to help you receive this divine love and to send you their love as well.

7) Allow the divine love to flow to each area of your body and to every cell that released the grief energy.

8) See, feel, or think about divine love filling each of these cells.

9) Thank your spiritual helpers for their assistance.

10) Thank yourself for bringing in this beautiful, healing energy.

The experience of receiving this powerful divine love into your heart center actually fills your heart with the energy of that light and elevates the vibration of your entire being. During the visualization you may see a very bright light or experience warm energy flowing into your chest cavity and throughout your whole body. It is a very simple process, and yet it has profound results because it creates a sacred moment of deep peace and healing.

Bringing in the divine love energy is the next important step in achieving the long-term goal of remembering your baby with love rather than pain.

Make Radiant Heart Healing Your Own

You can empower yourself by using these first two components of RHH for self-healing. Using this unique method allows you to take charge of your emotional heart, and you will find you are no longer a victim of your pain. Therefore, you can make a choice to stop suffering and open your heart to love once again—a powerful, life-affirming choice.

Repeat the RHH visualizations in components I and II as often as you feel the need. Grief and healing are different for everyone. If you are like most people, you will feel great relief after the first session, and then you will need to release again and again as new waves of grief wash over you. With practice, your heart will feel warm and full of love for longer periods of time. Eventually, the grief energy will be completely replaced with the energy of love.

It is important to *avoid recreating the feeling of grief* after completing the release work. The thoughts you have in the minutes and hours immediately following your session will determine whether you keep your heart filled with divine love or return to pain. You will likely find it much easier to remember your baby with love when the heaviness of your heartache has been released. The key is to focus your mind on the connection you have with your spirit baby who now resides in heaven and avoid thoughts of yearning to have your blessed infant back in physical form. Hold the vision of your spirit baby being happy and well cared for in a joyful place of infinite love.

It can be very helpful to read aloud and record the RHH visualizations in components I and II. When you play them back, you can relax and follow the steps with a clear mind. Another option is to work under the guidance of a certified Radiant Heart Healing practitioner. An updated list of practitioners is available at www.radianthearthealing.net.

III. Meaningful Spirit Communication

Spirit communication from infants occurs more often than most people realize. Those who experience it usually keep it a secret or reveal it to only a few trusted friends or family members, who are then sworn to secrecy. No one wants to hear, "It's just your imagination," or worse yet, "You're crazy."

Thankfully, times are changing, and spirit communication is becoming more widely accepted. More and more innovative psychiatrists, psychologists and grief counselors are supportive when their clients report feeling the presence of a loved one or receiving a message from one who has passed on. These sensitive, healing professionals recognize that such spiritual events can have a very positive, therapeutic effect.

Spirit communication from your infant on the other side may occur spontaneously while doing the visualizations for bringing in divine love. Spirit beings exist in realms filled with very high energies. When your energy field is uplifted by an influx of divine love, you will find it easier to pierce the veil and connect with your beloved infant.

Bringing in the energy of divine love also opens the door to an awareness of your baby's presence at other times. The spirit of your infant may come to you in a dream or contact you through a vision, a message, or even a familiar smell. You might experience moments of inspiration while meditating or going about your day-to-day routine. You can also receive communication through a friend, a stranger, or a spiritual medium. All of these sources are valid.

If the language of Spirit is unfamiliar to you, it is possible you will simply be unable to see, hear, or notice the messages your baby is sending to you. But the more you know and understand about the subtle ways spirit communication occurs, the more likely you will be able to receive those messages. So take heart—you can learn the language of spirit communication and open up a whole new range of possibilities for healing your grief.

Recognizing a message from your spirit baby is the third important step in achieving the long-term goal of remembering your baby with love rather than pain.

IV. Shifting to a Spiritual Perspective

I have found that people who hold certain beliefs have a much easier time healing after the loss of an infant. In general, these people have a positive view of a spiritual life that continues after the death of the physical body. To be more precise, they might say:

- There is no enemy called death.
- I am an eternal spirit.
- My baby is an eternal spirit.
- Spirit babies send signs and messages to loved ones on earth.
- These messages consistently say, "I still exist. I love you."
- Our family love bonds stretch into eternity.
- There is only love.

Some of these statements—or all of them—may already ring true. Or they may not. As you struggle to make sense of what has happened, chances are you will do some soul searching, read about new ideas, or learn from the experiences of others. I encourage you to consider ideas that are unfamiliar, and see if they might bring you comfort, or help explain some things that just do not make sense to you right now.

For most people, beliefs about life and death evolve to some degree over a lifetime. During periods of heightened spiritual or personal growth, our belief systems may shift significantly. Dealing with intense grief, as you are now, can facilitate profound growth and change.

Raising your consciousness by shifting to a spiritual perspective about life, death, and the afterlife is the fourth important step in achieving the long-term goal of remembering your baby with love rather than pain.

Transformation Through Radiant Heart Healing

You can use the Radiant Heart Healing process to clear your heart of pain, free yourself from suffering, and transform your grief into joy. This is a radical new message about healing grief! Can it be true?

Yes, I believe this statement is true. The stories that follow and the others found here and throughout this book are included because they provide evidence that supports this statement. The stories tell of the struggles, the insights, and in many cases, the spiritual transformations of others who have traveled the path of grief before you. Reading them with an open mind and an open heart will help you expand your beliefs about what is possible after the loss of an infant. For Sylvia, Kimberly, Sam, Ann and many others, the healing is deep, transformational and permanent.

Healing Recent Grief Due to Infant Loss

Radiant Heart Healing can be effectively used immediately after the death of an infant—however, this rarely happens. It is usually a few years before grieving loved ones are guided to work with me or other Radiant Heart practitioners. (Incidentally, my definition of "recent" grief is any time within five years of an infant's passing.) As you will see from these next two stories, each RHH session is as unique as the individuals who come for healing. Spirit guides the sessions and the divine love energy opens the door for healing to occur in many different ways.

The Triplets and Kimberly: Poetry From Heaven

Kimberly, the mother of triplets who lived for only a few hours after being born, did a Radiant Heart Healing retreat with me about a year after losing the babies. On our last afternoon, the sun on the water seemed to beckon, and I was inspired to work outside on my deck overlooking Lake Michigan. As we did the RHH visualizations in the glistening sunlight, a very slight breeze came off the lake, and nature sounds formed a backdrop of sweet, gentle music. The God-energy surrounding us was palpable.

At the close of the session, Kimberly sat absolutely quiet for the longest time; then she began channeling this message from her spirit babies.

We are the wind's gentle breeze,
The whisper in the wind,
The vibrant leaves blowing,
The birds' cheerful tune,
The ripple of the water,
The light of your life,
The love of your heart,
And so... remember us always.

This profound moment of spirit communication from Kimberly's triplets unfolded just as we finished using the RHH release visualizations and replaced her grief with the energy of pure love. As Kimberly opened to the divine, she became one with the trees, the sound of the waves against the shore, and the gentle breeze. At the same time, she became one with the spirits of her babies, and these beautiful, loving words flowed effortlessly into her mind and her heart. The poem seemed to write itself.

This was a mystical experience of deep healing and all-encompassing peace for this grieving mother. The peace of Oneness brought a knowing that the spirits of her babies are very much alive in a different vibration; yet, they are still connected to her. In that moment, there was no room for grief while her heart was filled with the tranquility of Oneness. As in the Inca tradition, Kimberly's spirit babies brought powerful medicine for healing their mother's grieving heart.

Star and Sylvia: A Message for Daddy

Sylvia and I met about two years after Star's transition. In this first RHH session, Sylvia wanted to focus on filling her heart with divine love, so we began by doing the visualizations for opening her heart and bringing in the bright light of spiritual love. Within seconds Sylvia announced, "Star is here. I can feel her presence, and I'm getting the special tingling feeling all through my body. The tingling comes whenever she's around."

Sylvia sat quietly in a meditative state as various images and symbols flowed into her inner vision. I sat with her, holding sacred space, and used visualization to send more divine light and love through my hands into her heart center.

I'm seeing a brilliant star out in front of me and up high to the left. That's Star's spirit for sure. That's always her signal to me.

112

This is fascinating! There's a bright beam of light coming from the star into my right eye. I wonder what it means. Oh, I see. She's reminding me that she could only see with her right eye because the left one was malformed.

Now I see a big mother lion. I wonder why Star is showing me this symbol. Oh, she is reminding me we are both Leos. Also, she's making me think of a big mother lion, and I'm getting the phrase, "fierce mother love." This is so cool! Star knows my love for her is fierce like a mother lion.

Now my spirit baby is showing me a photograph we took of her in the hospital. I see her beautiful, long hair. Most babies have no hair or very little hair. However, Star had a full head of blonde hair that was several inches long. The nurses all loved to stroke her hair. We don't have many pictures of Star, but this one is our favorite.

This next image coming in is rather vague. It looks like a doll in a green corduroy dress with long red curls—you know, those banana curls. Oh, wait. It's a picture of me when I was three years old. Why is Star showing me this? I don't get it.

Sylvia sat very quiet for some time with a puzzled expression on her face. Then this look of awe came over her face, and she burst into tears of joy as the message dawned on her. She announced with much excitement:

I got it! I know what Star is trying to tell me. Star's daddy loves these two photographs, and he carries them facing each other in his wallet. It's amazing that Star would send me a reminder of these two pictures! I can't wait to tell her father about this! I'm sure this is a message for him. She wants me to tell him she knows about those pictures in his wallet, and she's glad he carries them. She knows how much he loves her still. He doesn't recognize any signs from Star, so she is sending a message through me.

Now Star is showing me just one candle with a tiny flame burning. It's not on a cake or anything—it's just floating in front of me. Somebody blew out the flame. That's Star's way of saying goodbye. I felt her energy leave—my body isn't tingling anymore. She's gone for now.

Sylvia sat hugging herself for a time and enjoying the moment. She was all aglow with the divine love energy she felt coming from Star's spirit. After a few moments of silence, she ran to get the wallet from Star's father, who was in the waiting room. There were the two pictures that Star's daddy carries at all times—his reminder of the love he holds in his heart for his blessed spirit baby and her mother, who still lives here on earth.

Again, we see a spirit baby acting as a healer for her mother's grief and sending the gift of healing to her father as well. It is such a blessing that Sylvia is aware of her spirit daughter and can receive these messages that bring connection, joy, love, and peace. You might imagine that your spirit baby is close and has a desire to bring you healing just like Star, the other babies in this book, and the spirit babies of the Inca people.

Old Grief Is Just as Real

Radiant Heart Healing is also effective for clearing grief energy that has been stored for years. Millions of people who have suffered the death of an infant many, many years ago have never truly healed. Some are aware of their grief, while others have buried it so deep they don't even realize they have closed their hearts to deaden the pain. In either case, most of these people present a happy face—while inside they are slowly dying. Keeping up a façade like this is a very painful way to go through life.

Is your heart heavy with old grief? *If so, remember that it's never too late to heal your wounded heart.*

Brian and Sam: Healing a Father's Long-Term Grief

Twenty-seven years after losing Brian, Sam was introduced to Radiant Heart Healing and decided to have an individual session. His second son, Brian, was stillborn due to a diabetic pregnancy. Within six months, Sam's marriage ended and he moved to an apartment. He soon found himself reeling from multiple losses—he had lost his new baby, his marriage, his home, and his relationship with his five-year-old son. Sam spent many years exploring different ways to heal his devastating grief, yet he never felt totally clear.

> *Losing Brian was quite a blow. In the hospital my wife and I held Brian and cried together. Then, after the funeral, we both shut down, and didn't really talk to each other. When a baby dies in our culture, the mother gets all the attention. I felt like I was "just the father."*

> *For years after losing Brian, I couldn't hold a baby because it would bring up too much pain. Every time I would see a baby or a young child, I would think, "Oh, Brian would be about that age now." I do it even now, when I see a young man in his twenties.*

Each time, I get this bittersweet feeling. I've cried many tears over losing our baby, but I still carry some heartache.

Sam is sensitive to energy, so it was easy for him to sense the grief energy held in his heart and his body. He was able to see the grief energy as a dark green color and imagine releasing it. We finished by filling Sam's heart with divine love, and he announced with great excitement:

I see pink! That's the color, and it's all over the place! I can also feel pink. Everything is pink. It's inside my chest and all around in my aura. My entire vision is filled with pink energy.

I feel so alive. I'm very hot and tingling all over! I enjoy feeling alive. I don't enjoy feeling shut down. At the moment, I have the feeling of lightness. I feel quiet, peaceful and very light. That heavy, dragging-me-down feeling is gone. It's been twenty-seven years. I've had a remnant of inner turmoil that has haunted me all this time. It's not there anymore.

The strangest thing is happening. I can breathe again! My chest has expanded, and I can take a deep breath for the first time in years. I've been suffering with CPD (Chronic Pulmonary Disorder) for years, but I never realized the connection to my grief about Brian. This is fascinating!

Maryanna and Ann: Healing Secret Shame and Guilt

Ann began Radiant Heart Healing sessions seeking relief from the heartache of her mother's death. During our weekly sessions, she opened her heart, sent out the heavy grief energy, and filled her heart with divine love. Within a month, she felt great relief, and we began discussing other areas of her life. For some unknown reason, I felt guided to share with Ann that I was writing a book about healing grief after the loss of an infant. That was the opening for Ann to confide that she was still suffering from the loss of two babies—nearly forty years before.

Ann's baby girl, Maryanna, was pronounced perfectly healthy at her six-week check-up; yet, she died the next day of SIDS. Ann and her husband were in shock and deep despair for years afterwards. Ann's grief was compounded by the fact that she had not recovered from the heartache of having placed her newborn son Robbie for adoption the year before Maryanna's birth. She blamed herself, saying, "This is my punishment for giving up Robbie." Ann's guilt was overwhelming, and she spiraled into a depression that lasted almost four decades before she found relief.

I thought I had to be very strong and not show any of my emotions. I was extremely depressed, though I didn't really identify myself as depressed. Looking back, I had no feelings of excitement or joy for years and years. I actually felt like I didn't deserve anything good.

I couldn't stand to be around babies or a pregnant woman; in fact, I actually felt physically ill around any baby. It never occurred to me to seek help, so I lived with the misery, the secret shame of giving up my son, and the guilt of believing that everything was my fault.

I've had this recurring dream about Maryanna every few weeks for thirty-seven years. It began just weeks after her transition. In the dream, I'm giving my little girl a bath in the bathroom sink at home. I'm feeling quite disturbed as I'm washing her—and then I wake up. The dream is always the same, and each time I wake up with such terrible grief filling my heart.

After so many years of feeling disgraced, remorseful, humiliated, and full of self-reproach about Robbie and Maryanna, Ann used RHH to heal her grief at last, and then went on to transform her judgments about herself. Now she says:

I feel completely different about my life. I see these events from a completely different point of view. I have forgiven myself. I let go of my mistaken guilt, and I freed myself from my feelings of shame and dishonor.

I used to believe that people would hate me if they knew the truth about my life. Now it doesn't matter what others think. I am who I am! I'm at peace with myself, and I'm growing to love myself more each day!

My recurring dream has stopped, and I've opened my heart to loving the spirit of my baby in heaven. I've even had a few visions of Maryanna, and she's always dancing and laughing. It's so good to laugh again and feel free!

Laughter is always good medicine! Ann feels blessed to know that her spirit daughter is bringing the medicine of joy and laughter into her life.

The RHH sessions opened the door for Ann to have a spiritual awakening and begin to view herself and her life with soul eyes as well as human eyes. She was able to heal all her painful feelings after she did the release work, filled her heart with divine love, and then shifted to a spiritual perspective. Ann now sees herself through eyes of love.

♥   ♥   ♥

Summary of Chapter Eight

1) Radiant Heart Healing is a model of spiritual healing that is very useful for alleviating grief. It has four components:
   - Releasing the energy of grief from your heart.
   - Filling your heart center with the energy of divine love.
   - Having an experience of meaningful spirit communication.
   - Shifting to a spiritual perspective about life, death, and the afterlife.

2) The energy of grief has a low, slow vibration that weighs heavy on your heart.

3) You can use the power of your mind to visualize (imagine) or think about the grief energy leaving your heart, and the release will happen.

4) Divine love is the most powerful healing force in the universe. It has a high, fast vibration and is seen as an intense, bright light.

5) You can use your mind to visualize divine love flowing into your heart. This will empower you because you now have an effective tool for repairing your wounded heart.

6) Filling your heart with the energy of divine love raises your vibration and opens the door to the other side. This promotes an experience of communication with your spirit baby and brings the energy of joy, peace, and love into your whole being.

7) Your baby is an eternal spirit who is still bonded to family on earth and has the ability to send signs and messages to loved ones here. You can learn the language of spirit communication and open to a whole range of possibilities for healing your heart and uplifting your spirit.

8) Your spirit baby is a healer for your grief just as the spirit babies of the Incas bring healing for the mind, body, and spirit of the tribal people.

9) Many people carry grief for years and years after the loss of an infant, and while some never do heal, it is never too late to heal from this devastating life event.

10) The long-term goal of Radiant Heart Healing is to remember your baby with love rather than pain.

CHAPTER NINE

Additional Tools
for Healing Your Heart

My heart has a terrible ache that medicine can't take away.
—Darlene, Mother of Twins

It is true, there is no medicine for grief, and there is no quick fix. Does this mean you are doomed to carry your painful emotions forever? My answer is a resounding "No!"

You might want to check your beliefs about this subject. Perhaps you believe, *"I will never get over the heartbreak of losing our baby."* Most grief books support this idea and provide ways *to cope* instead of ways *to heal*.

In contrast, the premise of this book is: *You can completely free yourself from suffering and transform your grief into joy.* This somewhat radical new message is supported by story after story showing that transformational healing is possible after the loss of an infant. You will also be provided with proven ways to achieve this.

Coping or Healing?

The prevailing attitude in our culture is that we can—and should—learn ways to cope with our grief. Too often we put on a brave façade and carry on with our lives, yet never completely get over our loss. In fact, some people assume it is wrong to let go of grief completely, or worse, that to do so means dishonoring your loved one.

Perhaps you still feel a deep heartache when you remember your baby, but you have learned to go on with your life while keeping the pain at a manageable level. You still miss your baby's physical presence and yearn for what might have been, but you do your best to put the yearning out of your mind. All of this is a classic picture of coping.

Transformational healing, on the other hand, means you have stopped suffering and have transformed your pain into feelings of peace, joy and love. You have not forgotten your baby or the circumstances surrounding your loss, but you have learned to think of his or her birth and death in a new way. Reaching this level of healing is a step-by-step journey. It takes as long as it takes, but keep in mind that there is an end. You will know you have reached your destination when you can think of your infant and consistently feel love instead of pain.

Your healing journey will have many hills and valleys; using the Radiant Heart Healing process (see Chapter 8) will ease the way. Here are three additional tools that will make your journey smoother, easier, and faster:

1) Set an intention.

2) Clear your heart with crying and talking.

3) Make powerful choices—most importantly, a choice for healing over suffering.

Setting an Intention for Healing

Whatever you focus on gets bigger. It is a universal law of metaphysics that is always in effect for those who know this principle—and also for those who don't. Consider this: If you stub your toe, then sit down and focus all your attention on how painful it is, you may suffer for quite a while. If, instead, you stub your toe and immediately your best friend calls with a hilarious story about what happened to her on the way to work, you will give her your full attention. In minutes you will both be laughing yourselves silly—and when you hang up, you will realize your toe did not get such a bad bump after all.

When you make a conscious choice about where you focus your attention, you give energy to whatever you focus on and diminish whatever you ignore. This is not to say that by not thinking about your grief it will miraculously go away. Far from it. But it does mean that when you bring positive, healing thoughts to mind throughout the day, those thoughts will take root and begin to flourish. Let these positive thoughts become the compass for your healing journey. *The key is to make a choice to heal and set an intention to focus on the good in your life.*

Dillon and Stephanie: I Am a Survivor

After three years of infertility procedures, Stephanie and Mike were joyfully awaiting the arrival of their first child. However, at five months the ultrasound showed there was no amniotic fluid; Dillon's kidneys were greatly enlarged and not working. This, of course, was a death sentence.

Stephanie was heartbroken and spiraled into a deep depression. Her all-consuming thought was, "I would rather be dead so I can be with my baby."

Weeks after Dillon's transition, Stephanie's mother, a cancer survivor of fourteen years, felt moved to say to her daughter, "You are a survivor now. You have to learn what that means." These inspired words became the intention that guided Stephanie on her healing journey.

> *Becoming a survivor is not something I asked for, but now that I am one, I know I must embrace it. I realize Mom didn't ask for cancer, just as I didn't ask for Dillon to be taken away, but it is what it is. The facts are, she's a good person who got cancer, and I'm a good person who wanted my child to live more than anything on this earth, but he died anyway. So when Mom said those words to me, I realized that my life was going to change, regardless of my wanting it to or not. Mom gets it because she's lived it, and chose to make changes rather than stagnate. My goal is to do the same.*

> *What I've learned is that I must go on, and I have the power to choose how I go on. Will I be bitter? Or will I accept what happened and open my heart to forgiveness and love? Believe it or not, these were hard questions to answer at first. Even now I vacillate at times, but I know the answer.*

> *Doing my grief work is part of becoming a survivor of the events that come along in my life, so I must continue to do it. I've also learned that being a survivor means I am not in control. The sooner I learn to release what I can't control, the sooner I will receive peace.*

Marley and Bernadette: No Longer a Victim

Bernadette was thirty-five and thrilled to be pregnant with her first baby. But in the first few months she had a nagging feeling that all was not well. She was just starting to get past her concerns when, at twenty weeks, medical tests indicated that her baby girl was developing without a brain. Our interview took place just five months after Marley's transition, and Bernadette had already made some difficult but valuable choices about handling her loss.

> *My grief has been more than I ever imagined. It wrenched my heart with overwhelming anguish. The first month it was all-consuming; I decided to stop working and take some time to heal. I went to New York to spend a few days with family and friends. It was the best thing I could have done.*

I've been a mental health professional for quite some time. Consequently, I knew where this could go, and I didn't want to get stuck or lost in the grief. I knew it would be easy to fall into the role of a victim and allow negative thoughts to take over my mind. I also knew I had the power to choose another path and heal my grief. I made a decision to avoid going down the road of victimization.

I had to practice what I preach, keep moving forward, and find ways to get through the grief, hurt, and anger. It took the love of family, friends, and support groups to help me do that. I could not have done it on my own. One of the most loving statements came from a woman minister who counseled me. She looked deeply into my eyes as she said, "Marley has her own soul. She has her own journey. We don't know what her journey is." Peace filled my heart as I absorbed her words.

The stories told by Stephanie and Bernadette illustrate two very powerful intentions: *I am a survivor* and *I have the power to heal my grief.* Each of these women made a conscious choice to affirm the possibility of healing. This was the first step in an arduous, yet successful, healing journey. Of course, they each had many more steps to take, but stating an intention set both the direction and the destination for the journey.

Choosing Your Own Intentions

As powerful as these positive choices are, not making a choice can be just as powerful. It leaves the door open for more negative but commonly held beliefs about death and grief to dominate your thoughts. Many of these old beliefs do not serve you and can actually prevent healing. Well-meaning friends and family may even unwittingly reinforce these fatalistic ideas with clichés and oft-repeated platitudes. With the best of intentions, they might say things like:

- You will never get over the loss of your baby.
- You will always have a hole in you heart.
- Your endless grief proves how much you loved your baby.

Unless you consciously choose otherwise, these negative statements can, by default, become your unconscious intentions—your psyche will make them come true, and you will most likely become stuck in suffering. When you hold intentions like these, the best you can hope for is learning how to cope instead of how to heal.

But you can make a different choice. If you notice a negative thought in your mind or hear a sympathetic statement that suggests you'll carry this pain forever, fill your mind instead with your own powerful healing intentions to counteract these negative messages.

You may want to take some time over the next few days to list some healing intentions of your own. Write them down as positive statements. (That is, do not use words like "no" or "I won't" or "never." Instead say, "I intend to" or "I choose to," and so forth.) Also, state your intention in the present tense, as though it is happening right now rather than at some time in the future. Don't worry if your positive statement is not quite true yet, or even if you are not sure you believe it will happen. Your unconscious mind will respond to the statement you make, and in time your conscious mind will as well. Here are a few to get you started.

♥ I choose to completely heal my grief.

♥ My heart is whole again and filled with peace, joy, and love.

♥ I choose to stay connected to the spirit of my baby.

♥ I am finding people who listen deeply and support me.

♥ I attract all that I need to heal my grief—earthly angels, heavenly angels, books, songs, new friends, classes and healing groups.

♥ I choose to grow through and beyond this tragedy.

Manifesting Your Intentions

When using affirmative intentions, it is important to proclaim your choices again and again and again. Make a list of them and keep it in a place where you can see it often. You can say these intentions out loud or simply whisper them in your mind and hold them in your heart. Repetition is important in order to claim the power of your positive choice and overcome the old thought patterns that have programmed you to suffer rather than heal.

Affirmations are not magic, and repetition does not automatically produce the results you want. The key to achieving success is the emotional energy that you attach to your intentions. Attaching fear automatically blocks the possibility of completing your goal; it is important to understand that disbelief creates the energy of fear. Attaching the energy of excitement, joy, love, or peace to your intention will invite Spirit to deliver the outcome you are affirming. So the secret to manifesting your intentions is to hold the perfect scenario in your imagination and then invest this vision with the powerful energy of positive feelings. It is the energy of your pure, positive feelings that acts like a magnet drawing your heart's desires directly to you.

Clearing Your Heart With Crying and Talking

Love is the most powerful healing force in the universe. However, there is little room in your heart for love when it is filled with grief. My intention in writing this book is to provide guidance for anyone who has the courage to take the journey inward to the heart. As you move forward step by step, I invite you to keep your heart open, feeling and releasing your way through the grief so you can make space for love to flow in and work its miracle of healing.

Crying Is a Natural Way to Release

Grief is a very heavy emotional energy that resides in your heart—not in your head. Therefore, you cannot think your way through grief. John W. James and Russell Friedman, authors of *The Grief Recovery Book* explain it: "Grief is about a broken heart, not a broken brain. All efforts to heal the heart with the head fail because the head is the wrong tool for the job. It is like trying to paint with a hammer—it only makes a mess."

So if thinking about your grief will not make it go away, what will? The way to get over the heartache, despair, anger, grief, and all of your other painful feelings is to simply open your heart and release them.

Imagine you have a gash on your thigh that has healed over, but is badly infected deep within. You will need to open the wound and clean out the infection before healing can take place. Without this cleansing the wound will fester and get worse. Likewise, your heart is wounded, and your grief is an emotional infection. The grief energy needs to be cleared out so your heart can heal.

Crying is a natural way to release. Babies and little children usually express feelings very naturally through crying. They cry with vigor, so their emotional energy flows easily through open channels, often releasing as quickly as it started. They also scream with fear, yell out in anger, and shriek with joy. In their innocence, these youngsters have not yet learned to suppress, repress, or inhibit their emotions. We could learn much from watching their natural, free-flowing way with feelings.

Next time you feel a wave of grief rising up inside, find a safe place where you can cry loudly and not worry about other people's reactions. While in your safe place, allow the grief to rise up, wash over you, and then release it with a good, soulful cry. Let yourself be like a child—uninhibited, loud, and expressive. If you try to cry quietly, you are more likely to hold back, and so hold on to the grief energy. If it helps, think of it as deep crying, weeping, wailing, bawling, howling, bellowing, keening, or any other word that speaks to you of unabashed, full-throttled emotional release. Do it! Go for it! Be as loud as you need and want to be!

One very wise, grief-stricken mother described her need to cry after her baby's transition. "Crying is one of the healthiest ways to grieve. I love to cry and get the grief out, so I get out as many tears as I can. People ask me why I'm crying, and I say, 'I'm crying because I want to feel better. Just leave me alone and let me cry.'"

Pain and Love Intertwined

Another mother had this to say about struggling to release her pain after the death of their infant son.

I believe the soul of my baby resides in heaven. I also believe I have a connection to his soul, and the love we share will never die.

My therapist kept telling me I had to release my pain. I agreed this was a good idea, but I couldn't figure out how to do it. For so long, I found that the pain and the love for my baby were intertwined. When I was in the deepest part of my grief, it felt like letting go of the pain would mean letting go of the love. The very idea filled my whole being with an overwhelming fear. So, of course, I was stuck; I couldn't let go of the pain because I didn't want to give up the love.

It took me almost a year to learn that I could release the pain, yet keep all the love and my eternal connection to my son. That was a huge thing to learn!

Crying: Releasing vs. Recycling

It is important to understand that crying is an effective tool for releasing, but not all crying is beneficial. In the Radiant Heart Healing method I distinguish between two forms of crying—releasing and recycling. Understanding the difference between these two is crucial to healing.

Crying and releasing the energy of grief is key to healing your heart after any loss. Releasing means you are clearing the energy of your emotional pain completely out of your heart as well as the cells of your body. This is powerful crying! Indeed, you will feel empowered as you take charge of moving the grief energy that is weighing heavy on your heart.

When you are releasing, the soulful crying sounds start deep in your belly, move up through a channel in the center of your body, flow unrestricted through your throat, and are finally released out your mouth. The crying is strong, loud, hard, intense, and often quite painful while you are going through it. This kind of crying does not go on for hours; in fact, it often stops abruptly after fifteen minutes, or even less, because at some point the grief energy simply dissipates. After a good release, you will feel as if some kind of internal pressure has been relieved. Then a natural state of balance will return. You may even announce, "I feel lighter." For many people, laughter and joy bubble to the surface, and a feeling of peace is restored.

Crying and recycling the energy of grief feels completely different from releasing. Recycling means that while crying you are holding on to the energy of your pain and circling it through your body over and over again. Consequently, you do not receive the benefits of powerful crying; the pain does not vanish, and there is no sense of relief, peace, or joy as you finish. If you feel no relief when you cry, or if you actually feel worse afterwards, that may be because you are recycling your grief.

It's important to know when you are recycling. You might feel as though the crying comes from your throat rather than your heart or your gut, and it may sound more like a whimper than a wail. Without realizing it, you may be holding on to your grief simply because you feel hopeless and helpless. If so, there is a chance you will get stuck in your sadness and grind with it, rather than move through it to the end goal of release. Unfortunately, this kind of crying not only prevents healing but also promotes suffering. To achieve healing it is important to stop recycling your grief and make sure you are releasing this harmful energy.

Powerful crying (releasing) is very productive, and I encourage you to do it as often as you feel the need. Releasing is not a one-time thing, but rather a process that must be repeated over and over until the painful emotions subside. Each release experience is another step on your quest for healing your grief, and often it takes hundreds of steps for the journey to be complete.

Releasing your pain is much easier after you establish a strong intention to move from suffering to healing. Creating a passionate desire to love life in spite of your loss is also very important.

Cole and Danita: Shower Power

Cole's mother, Danita, cried every day for several months after losing Cole. At first, she experienced her grief as coming in waves that almost knocked her off her feet. Danita tried many ways to find her way through the most difficult times. She attended a few infant loss support groups, read books on grief, and accepted help from her many friends. She also went to a grief counselor for a short time because crying so much made her feel out of control. The counselor gave her a new way to look at the waves of grief by saying, "When you have the urge to cry, think of it as your son saying hello. It means you haven't forgotten him."

Danita found this thought very comforting. Afterwards, crying seemed much less threatening, and she was able to just let her tears flow. She even created her own powerful healing technique. It became her morning ritual and helped her immensely.

> *I can cry really hard in the shower. No one can see me, and I can just let the water wash away all of my bad feelings. The whole experience is very cleansing. When I finish, the sadness is done for the day. It's a brand new day, and I can go to work and function.*

Danita's shower technique is potent because it includes the intention of release and is supported by the action of the water flowing down the drain, carrying the pain along with it. It helps convey a great message to the psyche, because the grief is washed away and cannot be brought back.

Nellie and Meg: No End to the Tears

Meg, Nellie's mother, was suffering from severe depression when she came to my office five years after Nellie's death. Meg provided the perfect description of crying and recycling.

> *My whole world fell apart when Nellie strangled on the cord during labor and delivery. She was born blue. They tried to revive her, but nothing worked. At first I was in shock. I just couldn't believe this was happening to me. How could my baby be gone? What did I do wrong? I have never stopped blaming myself. Actually, I hate myself, and I think a lot about just ending it all.*

> *I used to cry my eyes out though I never felt any relief. It seemed like there was no end to the tears—if I let myself, I could still cry for hours. I hate being loud, so I cry as quietly as possible; actually I even try not to cry, but I can't seem to hold back the tears. People*

say it's good to cry, but I don't believe it. I think it makes my heart hurt even more.

Meg was surprised to hear that she was recycling her pain and thus experiencing no relief from her grief. We spent several sessions practicing release techniques such as opening her throat and making a loud tone as she imagined the emotional pain flowing up from her gut, through her torso, through her throat, and then out her mouth. With some coaching Meg learned to be passionate and loud about expressing her feelings; she then began to feel some relief, a sign that she had moved into powerful crying. After some practice, Meg learned to release the energy of the emotions she had been swallowing; her heart began to heal after all those years.

How Are You Crying?

I encourage you to notice how you feel after you cry. If you feel relieved, lighter, peaceful or joyful afterward, you are probably doing powerful crying. Keep up the good work! However, if you feel worse when you finish crying, you are probably recycling. Be gentle with yourself. You can learn to put more power behind those tears so you can release your pain instead of recycling it. The key is to cry hard for a short time and be loud about it. *Claim your right to release!*

Release Helps Heal Depression

Depression is the experience of viewing life through a dark filter. When you are depressed, life seems heavy, joyless, and burdensome. Creative energy and motivation are absent, and nothing seems to flow.

Depression is often defined as the absence of feelings. If you are depressed, you have made a choice (usually, unconsciously) to shut down and not be aware your feelings. This choice is a normal protective reaction to intense, overwhelming pain. This is the gift of going into shock and denial in the early days of loss. Trust that it is absolutely normal to experience deep depression in the first weeks—and even months—after losing a baby.

Depression, whether mild or deep, is a strong clue that you have painful feelings to release. Whenever you feel this way, I encourage you to open your heart, express your feelings, and release them. Then do it again—and again—and again. Each time you release the pain, it is important to fill your heart with love and focus on the good things in your life. *This simple formula is the way out of your depression.*

If this formula brings no relief, it may be beneficial to seek professional assistance. While fleeting suicidal thoughts are common after the loss of an infant and usually fade away as you move forward in life, persistent, ongoing suicidal thoughts are a red flag indicating it is time to seek help. There is no shame in asking for help through a grief support group or individual psychotherapy. In fact, the majority of people in these stories did seek some kind of counseling or participated in an ongoing support group.

A compassionate grief counselor can guide your healing journey and throw you a life raft as you swim through the sea of emotions that are common to this time of anguish. If the first counselor you see does not feel like a fit, try again. Counselors have different personalities and different styles, and it's important to have a sense of compatibility so you can trust enough to open your heart and heal.

Clearing Your Heart With Talking

It is extremely important to find a safe place to talk about your baby, your grief, and the signs and messages from your baby's spirit—indeed, your entire experience of going through the loss of an infant. Your haven may be a dear friend who has a big heart, a family member, a neighbor, or even a stranger who offers a shoulder to cry on. Discovering this safe place is more difficult than it sounds, because most people are uncomfortable with any grief situation, let alone the loss of a baby. Women I interviewed made these statements about finding a safe place to talk:

- "I never talked about my grief or my baby because nobody wanted to listen."

- "I couldn't talk to anyone in my family, so I buried it for twenty-five years."

- "The baby was a closed subject. Nobody ever spoke of her again."

- "I tried to talk to my husband, but he shut me out. It was just too painful for him."

- "I talk about my baby any chance I get. Lots of people give me strange looks when they hear me talking. I guess they are not used to a grieving mother talking about communicating with the spirit of her baby. Most people don't even know what to say."

Once again, locating a good grief counselor or an infant loss support group is one solution to the problem of finding a safe place. Counselors, as well as support group leaders, are trained to listen and be supportive while you express your feelings and talk about your grief. As one experienced grief therapist said, "The key to grief therapy is: Talk, talk, talk—cry, cry, cry—until it's over." Professionals are also trained to do more than listen; they can show you many skills, techniques, and tools that others have used to heal their heartache.

Talking, like crying, can be productive or non-productive. As you talk make sure that you are releasing your negative thoughts or feelings. Then shift your focus to the positives in your life. You can talk about your baby and your grief from an empowered position or a victim position; the latter is definitely non-productive. A victim statement is: "My baby's gone, and nobody can help me. Nobody understands what it's like to lose a baby." An empowered statement is: "I'm devastated to the core about losing my baby, but I will find a way out of this deep, dark hole."

Testimonials for Infant Loss Support Groups

Many of the mothers I interviewed for this book attended an infant loss support group as part of their healing journey. These quotes from three different mothers describe some of the important benefits of joining such a group.

Jessica, Mother of Danielle

I found my infant loss support group extremely helpful. The most important thing was that I no longer felt alone. I had people to talk to; we would talk about happy memories and sad moments with our babies. This group also provided a safe place for me to cry and just let it out.

Cheryl: Mother of Christopher

After Christopher died of SIDS, my therapist recommended I join a monthly infant loss support group. I resisted her suggestion for months and months because I'm a very private person, and I didn't like the idea of sharing my grief in such a public way. I couldn't imagine how it could be helpful. Boy was I wrong!

My group members were so supportive they became like family to me. No, better than family! I could express my deepest pain, and nobody told me I was crazy. Nothing was off limits. The older members showed me it was possible to heal; they gave me hope. That was the best part of being in group.

Kacie, Mother of Chandler

People outside my support group told me, "Just get over it. Go back to work." They really don't understand that healing grief is a process that takes time. You don't just flip a switch and get over it.

I'm working through the grief—not just getting over it. There's a big difference. People can bury all their feelings, go back to work, and appear to function. However, they are still carrying all their pain—they just pushed it down deep trying to forget.

I made a choice to express my heartache so that I can remember my baby with love in my heart rather than pain! It's not about forgetting, but getting to a place of love.

Finding an Infant Loss Support Group

When joining a support group, you need to be sure that the group facilitates moving through grief, as opposed to providing a place where people keep recycling their pain. Avoid groups that dissolve into a pity party, or reinforce the idea that you are a victim with no power to heal from the tragedy of losing your baby. Look for groups where the long-term members show definite signs of healing as opposed to continued suffering. Set an intention to follow their lead as you move forward on your healing journey. Again, each group is different, so you may have to try several groups until you find one that fits your needs and provides a healing environment for you.

I invite you to ask Spirit for guidance in your search for a local infant loss support group. Trust that you will be directed to find the assistance you need. You might begin by calling a local church, hospital, or funeral home and asking if they sponsor such a group. You can also check the yellow pages for grief psychotherapists or use the Internet to find national infant loss programs with a local chapter. Look for synchronistic signs and listen carefully for messages that might come through a friend or family member. A list of Grief Resources is provided at the end of this book.

Making Powerful Choices

As a soul, you came to earth with free will. The Creator has given you this most precious gift, and you create your life through your choices. You also learn through your choices. You are here in this physical world to learn to design a life that is joyful, harmonious, and filled with love. Even after the loss of an infant, it is possible to achieve this goal by making powerful choices.

You already choose everything you think, feel, and do in every moment. For most people this is usually an unconscious process. However, becoming a conscious chooser will empower you. Ultimately, this is how you can overcome feeling victimized by the challenges you face as you go through life. When you make conscious, powerful choices about your thoughts, feelings, and actions, life gets easier and flows more smoothly.

Some of the things that happen to you are beyond your control. Your baby left unexpectedly, and you had no choice about that event—you could not stop it, postpone it, or change the circumstances. No matter what out-of-control circumstances caused your loss, you do have a choice about how you respond to that tragedy, both in the moment and for the rest of your life.

Making a Choice to Focus on Positive Thoughts

Most people believe they have no control over what they think. They see their thoughts as a herd of horses running wild. But the truth is that you choose every thought you have. Currently, this choosing is an unconscious process, which is why you believe you cannot control it.

By bringing your awareness to this phenomenon, you have already taken the first step toward picking up the reins of that herd of wild horses. The next step is to learn to notice your thoughts as they arise. Below are ten examples of negative thoughts and their opposites. As you read them, notice which of them most closely resembles your usual thought patterns.

1) I hate my life and everyone around me.
   I am grateful for my life and all the people in it.

2) I want to isolate myself and avoid talking to people.
   I open my heart to receiving all the love and support flowing to me right now.

3) I will never get over this grief.
   My grief experience is an opportunity for personal and spiritual growth. I can find ways to grow and overcome this grief.

4) My baby's death has to be a mistake. Life is not fair.
   There are no mistakes. My baby came and went according to a bigger plan.

5) There is no way out of this terrible pain.
   I can find ways to release this pain and heal more and more each day.

6) God has abandoned me.
   My prayers for finding ways to heal are being answered.

7) This is too much pain. I want to be with my baby in heaven.
   I won't always feel this way. I choose to heal my grief and live my life with joy.

8) I will miss my baby until the day I die.
   Missing my baby can motivate me to connect with him or her in the spirit world and continue our relationship in a new way.

9) Death is the end of everything.
   There is no death at the spiritual level. My baby still exists in heaven.

10) Life is about suffering, and I am doomed to suffer the rest of my life.
    I will survive this, overcome all of my pain and suffering, and find joy again.

If the negative thoughts on this list seem more familiar to you than the positive ones, imagine what will happen as you begin to take charge and choose to focus on positive thoughts.

Making a Choice to Create Positive Feelings

Feelings follow thoughts. Consequently, negative thoughts create negative feelings and positive thoughts create positive feelings. This concept is very important in the process of healing grief. Minute by minute, you create your emotions by choosing your thoughts.

We learn many lessons through pain. For instance, when you touch a hot stove, it creates pain, so you learn not to touch it again. You can learn the same lessons about your thoughts. When a thought creates hurt, the best thing to do is this: *release the hurt, and do not touch that thought again.* It takes some discipline, but it is absolutely worth the effort.

There will be times when you miss your baby, and your heart is filled with grief. When this happens, you can release the grief using the Radiant Heart Healing visualizations. You can clear your heart with powerful crying. Or, you can talk or journal about your feelings. Whatever your approach, it is important afterwards to choose thoughts that bring joy, peace, or love.

This simple formula (release the negative, focus on the positive) creates profound results. Repeating this process again and again will eventually bring complete healing to your heart. It is easier to succeed when you give up old habits of thinking negatively. With practice, you can establish new habits that will help you move forward more quickly on your healing journey.

Harrison and Sharon: A Choice to Be Happy

Sharon, Harrison's mother, made an important shift in consciousness several years after his death.

My whole life I held a belief that I did not deserve to be happy, and losing Harrison was more proof that this was so. Happiness was just too much to ask. I thought, "If I ask for gladness, joy, and contentment, I'm being greedy."

Then one day I somehow got a little taste of being happy. The next day I went to Harrison's gravesite and had a long talk with him. I said to him, "I love you so much. My heart is always so full of love for you and from you. I've made a choice about my life. I deserve to be happy."

That was two years ago, and since that day my life has turned around completely because I set an intention to have joy in my life. I started making decisions based on the belief that I deserve happiness, and it's up to me to create it.

Soon after that, I realized it was best to divorce Harrison's father because I hadn't been happy in my marriage for many years. Right away, I met a new man and we fell in love. We have created a beautiful, loving family, and we have a new baby named William. I get to stay home and be a full-time mother to my older living son and William. I couldn't be happier. This all happened as soon as I quit punishing myself. I changed my belief, and all of a sudden, Spirit said, "YES!"

Spirit babies consistently send messages urging loved ones here on earth to be happy. So we can just imagine Harrison's great delight as he watches his mother manifest more joy and love in her life.

♥   ♥   ♥

Summary of Chapter Nine

1) Achieving transformational healing means you have stopped suffering and converted your grief into peace, joy and love. Also, you will be able to consistently think of your infant with love instead of pain.

2) You can truly heal your grief as opposed to simply coping with your heartache.

3) Consciously setting an intention to overcome grief will begin the healing process. The very act of making this decision is an empowering first step.

4) You can clear your heart of pain with powerful crying and talking.

5) Deep healing requires that you release—not recycle—the energy of your grief.

6) Recycling your pain keeps you stuck in suffering and prevents healing.

7) After clearing your pain, it is important to fill your heart with the energy of love, thereby uplifting your spirit.

8) Peace, joy, and love always exist beneath the grief. Trust that these feelings will emerge as you open your heart and let go of your pain.

9) Seeking professional assistance from a compassionate grief counselor or joining an infant loss support group is often beneficial.

10) Powerful healing choices include consciously keeping your focus on uplifting thoughts and intentionally creating positive feelings.

CHAPTER TEN

———∾∾∾———

Finding the Gifts in the Tragedy

Miranda gave me the gifts of growth, compassion, and gratitude.
She also taught me to try to live every moment
to the fullest. I'm sure she will continue
to bless my life with ongoing gifts
until we are once again together on the other side.
—Monica, Miranda's Mother

There are always hidden gifts in the grief loved ones experience after the death of an infant. Learning to find these gifts is essential to achieving transformational healing—a state in which you are able to think of your beloved infant and consistently feel love instead of pain. Indeed, discovering the gifts and embracing them shifts the outcome of your grief journey from coping to healing.

Viewing your loss with soul eyes is the key to finding the gifts in the tragedy of miscarriage or infant death. It may take weeks, months or many years before you have healed enough to do this. Give yourself as much time as you need. Trust that you will do it when you are ready. While you are waiting, have faith that when you begin to see with soul eyes, you will find peace, love, and joy beneath your devastating heartache.

My friends Ron and Denny Reynolds are spiritual teachers, healers, and the authors of a book entitled *The New Perspective*. In this book, they have coined the term "perspective shifting," and they offer these words of wisdom.

> *Perspective shifting is seeing with love, rather than viewing a situation through the eyes of fear. Shifting to the new perspective is finding the blessing in the experience and using it to grow. It's surrendering your victimization and reclaiming your power as a co-creator, remembering that life doesn't happen to you, but through you. Perspective shifting allows healing to occur.*

After the loss of an infant, everyone involved has the opportunity for perspective shifting. This change is an essential step on the path of spiritual growth; it allows healing to occur. But it is not automatic—it depends on the choices you make. When you are able to shift your perspective from human eyes to soul eyes and discover the gifts in the tragedy, it is easier to find new meaning in your life and heal at a much deeper level.

I invite each of you to use the following stories as inspiration for your own perspective shifting. When you are able to find the hidden gifts in your own grief experience, it will be easier to remember your beloved baby with love instead of pain.

The Gift of Transformation

The death of an infant shakes up your whole world and invites you to change your priorities after the initial time of confusion. As you move through the grief process, you will probably see your life with new clarity. Consequently, dealing with the death of a baby often becomes the catalyst for transformation. The following stories illustrate different kinds of transformation that took place for several mothers interviewed for this book.

Sally: Cherishing the Gift of Life

Sally lost her precious twins on Christmas Eve, just days before they were due. She sees the stillbirth of the twins as a defining moment in her life.

The loss of the twins was a real wake-up call for me. It made me look at life as a gift and see how precious it is that I get to take each and every breath. I decided to cherish this gift and do the best with my life that I could. Most importantly, I decided not to let anyone abuse me anymore.

My grief was the catalyst to go to therapy. It was the best decision I ever made! My goal for therapy was to get help for my grief and figure out why I was in this abusive relationship with William, the father of the twins. I desperately loved this man though we never married; we had some good times over the ten years that we were together. However, William was extremely negative, given to bouts of depression, drank way too much, and verbally abused me. I realized I was with him because I felt sorry for him. William was needy and I was the caretaker.

Losing the twins was the worst and the best thing that ever happened to me. It's now fifteen months past that fateful Christmas Eve. My life has taken a total turnaround. I broke off with William, and three months later, a new relationship came into my life. Robert treats me with respect and kindness—the way a woman should be treated.

Now I think I'm living a dream! I feel so blessed and so happy. I like to think the twins are up in heaven guiding me and cheering me on as I make all these changes.

Harrison and Grandma Fran: Love Changes Your Perception

Eight years after Harrison's death in the NICU, his grandmother Fran wrote this article for an infant support group newsletter.

For the past eight years, the time from November to March has been a different time for my daughter Sharon and me. My grandson Harrison was born in November and returned to heaven four months later. The miracle of his birth was followed by four months of joy, sadness, faith, hope, despair, anger, laughter, and tears. But most important, it was a time filled with love.

Families, friends, and strangers were brought together by the love this tiny child brought into this world. When he left us, that love remained—forever connecting us to him and each other. Eight years later, Harrison's brief life and his love are still touching people. That was his gift—the gift of love—to us all.

As I wrote this I started to say those months every year are a "difficult time," but then I realized that "difficult" is not the right word. Yes, it is difficult to remember that I cannot hold him in my arms or watch him grow up. It is also difficult when I feel my heart break from the pain of remembering.

It was easier to close my heart, to shut out the memories, to not feel anything. Then life was not so difficult—at least on the surface. I went through days, nights, and even years on autopilot. Family, friends, and coworkers smiled and said how nice that I was getting on with my life. Inside, in my heart, the pain of the loss was still there.

Then one day I realized something had changed; I had changed. I had received another gift from Harrison—the gift of remembrance. I began to remember everything from waiting for his birth to having to say goodbye—and my heart didn't break. Instead, my heart opened and love surrounded all the memories. Love truly changes your perception and your life. It is no longer difficult to remember—instead, it's a joy to remember Harrison with love.

I had a special heart connection with Harrison that is still there today. He makes his presence known in our lives, and I know he watches over all of us. I am forever grateful for the two precious gifts he gave me—the gift of love and the gift of remembrance.

Individual Transformations Within a Support Group

Seven women from the Chicago area who were dealing with grief at the same time ended up together in a grief support group sponsored by Share, a national organization for healing grief after infant loss. Here they each describe the various gifts they found while seeking a solution to their grief.

Beth: Gifts of Compassion and Empathy

After the loss of her first and only baby, Beth opened her heart and became a more compassionate, loving person.

I see the gifts Josh's death brought to me—compassion, empathy, and all the loving people I've met. If God came to me and said, "You can turn the clock back before his death," I don't know that I would.

Losing Josh probably saved my marriage. My husband and I had grown apart, and the death of our son became an intense bonding experience for both of us. We supported each other through the grief and became closer because we were able to share our joys and pains, our ups and downs. I know many couples split up after the loss of a child, but we did the opposite. We renewed our commitment to each other, and our love grew.

Wendy: I Have Never Been So Close to God

This young mother has given birth to two living children and miscarried four other babies.

I miss the four babies I miscarried—that's for sure. They have given us soooo much that I can't even articulate it. What greater gift than to give their lives? That's the beauty of all their little souls.

It's hard to say what I would do if I had a choice between my life now and the babies. I think I would choose this life I have now—I don't know that I would choose the babies. I have never been so close to God, and I've been on this path for a long time. I would never have looked at a child the way I look at my two living children now.

My mother was a rather cold woman, and I would have been more like her had God not given me the gifts of these four miscarried children. Maybe they did give their lives over for something bigger. I never thought about that idea before.

Dawn: New Compassion Ripples Out

This wise mother described the ripple effect caused by her changes after the death of her beloved baby.

I'm a more compassionate person after losing our baby. My new compassion affects one person at a time, and then ripples out. Our kids are going to be different people—their kids are going to be different. It takes time, and it ripples out.

Maybe I've gone through this so I can help other people. People call me all the time when a friend or relative has lost a baby. They ask me what to do. I tell them to follow the person's lead—if they want to talk or feel, then listen to them. I also tell them it's important to remember the baby's father; he has feelings too.

Heidi: After a Slow Healing Process

Another mother expressed great words of wisdom about the time needed to find the gifts in the tragedy of grief.

Eventually your grief turns to joy, but it takes time. No matter what kind of loss you've had, you don't come out of it right away jumping for joy. You need to go through these phases, and you need to make it work for you. Each person needs to figure out how to make it okay. After a slow healing process—one step at a time—then you can find the gifts.

One of my gifts is that I'm a much better mother because of losing Brittany. I know how precious my living children are, and I definitely put them first. I'm also much more patient as a mother. Another gift is that I have a deep motivation to go back to school to get a nursing degree. Now I know I have an ability to help others, and I want to do that as a nurse. It's all because of Brittany.

I would be a very different person if I hadn't lost Brittany. I kind of like the way things are. I'm happy with how it's all worked out. If you are open to this idea and work through the process, you eventually get there.

Darlene: Gratitude and a Stronger, Deeper Marriage

Darlene contributed these comments ten years after the loss of their twins.

> *The biggest gift in losing the twins is that my husband and I bonded during the grieving process, and our marriage became stronger and deeper. Of course, in the beginning we were both so torn apart we couldn't even connect; but after getting through our grief, we got closer.*

> *Larry and I are the only ones who know exactly what we have been through as parents of twin babies who died. Nobody, not even the grandparents, can really know how it was for us—it's like our little secret. Somehow we are very connected in the memories of our healing. It's been ten years, and we are at peace.*

> *Losing the twins has increased our sense of gratitude. That may sound strange, but it's true. After losing three babies (the twins and another miscarriage), we so appreciate our daughter Geneva, who at five years old is such a joy in our lives. We will never take her for granted! We are also grateful for our home, our friends, and our loving relationship.*

Tracy: The Gift of Group Love and Support

Peter's mother, Tracy, talked about the gifts she discovered during her healing journey.

> *One of the important gifts I received was the love and support in our Share group. When we have a memory held just within ourselves, the emotions associated with it get all bottled up. During our meetings, I could share whatever I wanted without censoring my thoughts and words; my personal expressions were accepted. It was my perception of my experience, and no one told me not to think or say anything, so I felt supported and validated in my feelings.*

> *It was also good to know I wasn't alone; others had been through an infant death and survived it. I had the opportunity to support, accept, and love others as they revealed their innermost thoughts and feelings of their own loss. Each of us was on our individual journey of grief, but we felt supported by the whole group as we walked our paths.*

> *I'm not the only one to know my son Peter, because I was also able to share every memory of him, every nuance of my pregnancy experience, and each part of the Peter that I knew. Now there is*

a whole group of wonderful people who also hold a memory of my Peter! I'm so happy that other people know him through my experience of him. Peter lives with us in my heart. Now, because of my Share group, he lives in many hearts—he goes on.

Monica: The Gifts Are Still Coming

Miranda's mother, Monica, is very aware of the gifts she received from her infant daughter who was stillborn. (See Chapter Thirteen for more of Monica's story.)

Miranda, my beautiful daughter who never took a breath, gave me the gifts of growth, compassion, and gratitude. She also taught me to try to live every moment to the fullest. I feel blessed because the gifts are still coming, and it's been ten years since her birth. I'm sure she will continue to bless my life with ongoing gifts until we are once again together on the other side.

Being together in this support group was a very bonding experience for these seven women, and after ten years they still maintain deep love for each other and for the spirits of their babies. The group interaction allowed all of them to change faster because they had the benefit of learning from one another. They each accomplished great personal transformation, shifted to a spiritual perspective about life and the afterlife, and found many gifts as a result.

The Gift of Oneness

Oneness is an experience of expanded consciousness when the veil of mystery dissolves between this earthly world and the spiritual world. The experience can last for a few seconds, a few minutes, a few hours, or it can extend for days. Whenever anyone expands into this miraculous state, they describe it in glowing terms. This expansion is a moment of spiritual awakening—a moment of connecting with the God-energy. It's a moment of seeing the spiritual truth of our existence. We are so much more than mere mortals with a human body and a personality. We are beings of light. We are made of divine love. So the Oneness might also be called heaven, the afterlife, Home, the Light or "the sea of divine love."

Lane and Heather: He Is Pure Love Energy

Heather, mother to three angels, has an innate ability to feel things in the spirit world—that place where the vibrations are too high to be experienced with our ordinary five human senses.

I lived at the Ronald McDonald House for six weeks while Lane was in the NICU. All the staff there supported me and went to see Lane at the hospital. They all just loved him! I tell you, my child's presence still lingers there in that house. The second I ring the doorbell and walk in, I can feel him so strong. His energy is overwhelming, and he's all around me. I feel like he's right behind me, and if I turned around quick enough, I'd see him.

Whenever I go to the Ronald McDonald House, I can feel Lane down to the depth of my soul. He is pure love energy. His energy is on my skin, inside me, in the air I'm breathing, and just everywhere. It's like being on a natural high! It's like no other feeling I've ever had. All my stress goes away and everything flows; then this peace comes over me, envelops me, and fills my whole being. It's such a beautiful experience!

I don't get this feeling anywhere else—not even at the cemetery. Lane was never physically present in that house, but that doesn't matter. I had a thousand conversations with him while I was resting in my room, and he was in the hospital across the street. He didn't have to be awake for me to communicate with him because his spirit could come visit while he was sleeping. His spirit was always present with me when I lived at the house, and his spirit is still present with me now when I visit.

Whenever I feel down, I drive over to the Ronald McDonald House just to get this feeling one more time. Lane has never let me down. Every time I go, I can feel him there and I get on this high. A friend of mine called this feeling "spiritual bliss." That describes it exactly!

Heather is obviously very intuitive and wisely uses her ability to connect with Lane's spirit as a way to heal her grief. Each time she goes to the Ronald McDonald House, she moves out of the low, slow vibration of grief and into the higher, faster vibration of divine love.

Heather has found an easy way to lift her spirits (raise her vibration), and she takes responsibility for doing so whenever she feels the need. Returning to the house is an empowering choice for Heather because it's a guaranteed way for her to create positive feelings. Heather is obviously letting her feelings be her guide—a very soulful way to live!

As souls, we each come to earth with the universal purpose of overcoming human challenges and then creating a life filled with joy, peace, and love.

Heather shows us it is possible to attain this goal—even after a beloved baby goes to the other side.

Harrison and Sharon: Sharing Love in the Oneness

Sharon, Harrison's mother, believes her baby opened the door to the divine and gave her a glimpse of heaven. Here are her words.

We all knew it was time for Harrison to make his transition. I was bawling so hard; I just kept crying and crying. At some point, I finally gave up all my hopes and dreams for Harrison. The second I let go, these extraordinary things began to happen. First, I felt this incredible presence near me. I looked up, expecting to see Christ. I didn't see Him, but I knew He was right there with us; I could feel His energy.

I was holding Harrison against my heart as I told him, "It's okay. It's time. Go with Christ. Don't hold on for Mommy." The second I said this, a feeling of great love came over me.

As this divine love washed over me, I went into a state of bliss. No, it was beyond bliss! It was a place beyond human thoughts and feelings. My mind had no worries—just total peace. Suddenly, I was one with everything! I was connected to everything and everyone. It was the best feeling ever. I felt such unconditional love in the Oneness. That's all I could feel—just total divine love.

Later a priest told me, "The time of transition is always sacred. Others have described this same state of bliss. Harrison opened a doorway to the divine. It's a gift from God to be able to have this little glimpse of heaven." My heart told me Harrison would be okay, because he was forever with Christ in this magnificent energy of divine love.

Strangely, for the first few days after Harrison's transition, I was so happy. I was still experiencing the bliss. I kept thinking, "I shouldn't be this happy." This whole experience was definitely not what I expected. It was such a paradox to feel such joy when moments before I was in the worst pain I'd ever felt in my life. How could that be? It made no sense to me.

No matter what, I want that feeling again. There was only love without judgment; everything unpleasant was gone. I know I will feel the Oneness again when I cross over. However, I don't want to wait that long. Sometimes now I can tap into all the love that's possible; I can feel everyone's love. It is always there for all of us, because it's something that's in all of us. Everyone is connected by this love. Of course, people have choices. They can choose to embrace the love and comfort or not.

Harrison is still part of me, and he always will be. We are connected in love; we are together in the Oneness. Whenever I think of this, I experience joy all over again. It seems like a paradox—feeling joy about my baby who transitioned to the other side. I don't feel joy about our loss; I feel joy about sharing love in the Oneness.

After weeks in this state of bliss, the feelings of love, peace, and joy began to dissipate, and I found myself in the worst heartache I've ever experienced in my whole life. Then, I had to deal with all the human emotions people have after losing a baby. It was so terribly painful, but I'm sure the memory of the bliss softened it some.

Since this experience with Harrison and Christ, my fears about death have simply vanished. In fact, I look forward to the time when I can once more experience the wonder of being on the other side with the God-energy.

For Sharon, the memory of being in the Oneness carries an enormous power and has promoted a shift in her understanding of God and the afterlife. Because of this experience, Sharon raised her consciousness to a much higher level; this is the core definition of healing. It was a time of great spiritual growth for her, and she is still awed by her experience.

The Gift of Finding a New Spiritual Purpose

Grief is the catalyst for many people to discover a new spiritual purpose. So how do you find this purpose? The ideas about your spiritual purpose come from your soul, and they trickle down into your consciousness through little glimmers of inspiration, intuitive knowings, and flashes of joy that light up your heart. All three of these are the whispering voice of your soul trying to get your attention.

Following your passion will also help you discover your purpose. Dr. Paula Hardin writes in *Love After Love*:

Finding out what your heart yearns for, and then expressing this goes far beyond how you earn money—it refers to who you are and what you must do. As you grow more in touch with your essential self, or your soul, your purpose infiltrates every aspect of your life. You could call this process a quest or calling, a passion or mission—it becomes your destiny.

After the loss of an infant and healing their own grief, many feel called to use what they have learned to discover their destiny—also known as a soul mission or soul purpose. Often, but not always, this mission includes a burning desire to assist others who are healing after a grief experience.

The following stories are a testament to the strength of the human spirit and they illustrate that it is, indeed, possible to discover your mission as you heal your grief about your baby.

Lane and Heather: We Do This Work Together

After losing three babies, Heather has become very aware of her soul mission here on earth, and she carries it out with great passion.

I spent months at the Ronald McDonald House while Lane was in the NICU. Even while Lane was still struggling to live, I could always feel his spirit with me at the house. I talked to him all the time and felt like he brought me comfort. Lane's spirit is still very present at the Ronald McDonald House for a reason. I believe he brings comfort to the other parents who come to stay there. That's his purpose now. He came and left so we could both do this work of helping other parents.

While I was visiting the NICU, I met another family with a baby named Lane. Their baby was much smaller, so we called him Little Lane. I got close to his mother during our time together in the hospital. Little Lane passed over three weeks before our son. His mother was crying as she said, "I'll never be able to have another baby." I gave her a business card for the doctor I love at the high-risk pregnancy center. She went to him and they just had a healthy baby boy! I feel so good that I was able to connect her with this special doctor.

I also started an Internet chat room for people who have lost babies. My Internet name is Dixieangel. One day, I was interacting in the chat room when Glenda sent me an instant message saying, "Do you have time to talk?" She wanted to talk about her baby Christian, whom she had miscarried a year earlier. We typed back and forth for some time before I told her that I'd lost three babies myself. She felt safe reaching out to me because I had angel on the end of my name. As we finished, she said, "I've been praying for help. You are the angel God sent to help me. I just know our babies brought us together."

We now have about one hundred women online in the chat room I started. I would say ninety percent believe their babies are alive in Spirit and are sending signs and messages. They believe because they have all had experiences; they share many of their heartwarming stories with me because they know I believe, also.

Last week, Cynthia told me she sat in her car crying by a lake, and a butterfly came and stayed on her windshield for over an hour. She believes it was a sign from her baby. I told her this was absolutely true!

These grieving mothers miss their babies deeply and long for communication with them. I tell them, "It can happen. You have to believe! Be open to getting a message, and when you do, embrace it. Enjoy it! You're not crazy. It's really, truly happening!"

Star and Sylvia: If It Weren't for Star…

Star's mother, Sylvia, studied several different spiritual teachings years before her baby's short stay on earth. Consequently, Sylvia was spiritually awake and able to discover some of her soul purpose within months after Star's transition.

My grandmother always said, "Every bad thing always happens for the good." I'm finding that so with my Star experience. If it weren't for Star, I wouldn't be where I am right now.

After she died, I was so sad and didn't have any energy. I would just sit on the couch, staring into space. One day, I felt her saying, "You can't just sit here and be depressed forever." She pushed me to go out walking and then inspired me to notice a nearby beauty school. It was never anything I was particularly interested in, even though I have a lot of artistic talent.

It turns out I'm a natural! I graduated and I just love my job as a cosmetologist and hairdresser. I didn't have any plan for my life after high school and would probably have been just working at any old job to pay the rent if I hadn't been inspired by Star. I thank her all the time for helping me to be where I am right now.

One of the great parts of working so up close and personal is that I'm very sensitive to other people's moods and energies. I can tell if they are up or down. I'm not very bashful, so I get right in and start asking questions. People usually thank me in the end.

Somehow, lots of parents who have lost a child end up at my station. One day it was six out of seven clients! I did nothing to make this happen. People usually ask if I have kids, and I always say, "I have an angel up in heaven." That day, my clients kept saying, "Me too." One mother had a son who died in a car accident and another's son committed suicide.

I always ask them to share their stories, and I tell them mine. Talking stories is so healing, and it lets the memory of our children live on. I think I get those people for a reason, even though they are assigned randomly to four operators as they come into the salon. It was just one after another that day. It was amazing!

I think everything we do in our lives prepares us for something bigger—something greater. When I was in the eighth grade, I began to read spiritual books and study about spiritual things. I learned about the power of positive thinking. You can push yourself forward, and you can overcome anything if you put your mind to it. Learning that and practicing it has helped me with my grief about Star. So many of the other things I learned have helped me too—like keeping your mind-body-spirit in balance and moving into harmony with everything around you. I know I will eventually become one with all of everything around.

I believe that everything we learn and all the life-changing events help us manifest who we are going to become and what's going to happen next in our lives. It helps us create our own destiny if we are able to open our eyes wide enough to see it. There's even going to be more; I'm sure I have even bigger things coming in the future. I see that my job is leading me to dream about what comes next for me!

I'd like to be a counselor for young women who have lost their children; I want to focus on ages twenty-five and younger. It's much different when you're only eighteen. People don't expect you to have children until you are a little older and married. I wasn't any of that. So yeah, all of this is just the beginning, and I owe it all to Star.

Emily and Diane: Together We Bring Healing to Many

Emily was born weighing only two pounds yet she lived for seven months. This tiny infant had a profound effect on many people even though she never left the NICU. Her mother, Diane, had a special glow about her face as she shared her sacred story of mystical experiences, healing grief, awakening to Spirit, and finding her mission in life.

Emily gave me the gift of connection—she taught me to look at life in a new way and see how connected and interconnected we all are. It's just so amazing to be able to see it! Maybe when I was younger, I never paid attention—for whatever reasons, I just didn't notice. But after Emily, I've come to believe that all people and events are interrelated. These days, I always look for the divine connection in everything.

The whole experience with Emily was so spiritual. I always felt like we were on some kind of journey with this baby and didn't know where it was going to end. In my heart I believed from the beginning that she wasn't going to be with us very long. I always thought it was weird but somehow, I just knew. For whatever reason, Emily was only meant to come and do the things she had to do; she was never meant to stay.

Right now Emily would be nineteen years old. That's a long time. Talking about her now makes me really happy. Of course, it wasn't always that way; the first few years were filled with agony. Then I gradually began to heal. From the beginning, I made up my mind to use my grief to expand myself, to get through it and get over it. Dealing with Emily in this way has made me more resilient. When you start out, you feel like it's not possible to ever heal. But it is! At first you feel like you shouldn't be laughing—you shouldn't be doing a lot of things. But eventually it feels okay. I've learned a lot from my experience with our daughter—important spiritual things.

I went to the hospital every day to visit Emily. I didn't quite understand it, but I felt a presence there—it was always so peaceful. I didn't know why, but a feeling of grace always surrounded this baby. I developed a routine of attending Mass before each visit, so I was in a spiritual state at my daughter's bedside. Thinking about it now, I know Spirit led me to do that so my vibrations would be really high when visiting Emily. Really! I was making myself "good" to be in the presence of everything there that was holy.

One day my Charismatic Catholic aunt came with me to the NICU. She told me she saw Mother Mary next to Emily's isolette, holding my sweet baby girl in her mantle. That was a holy moment! It was then I began understand it was Mary's presence I was sensing when I sat with our baby.

Emily constantly attracted perfect strangers to her bedside. We'd get off the elevator and find people gathered around her. Visitors would come to see another baby, but they would stop and talk to our daughter. Some would even reach in and stroke her little arm. I never knew these people, but the nurses used to say, "Everybody knows Emily, so they keep stopping by to see her." I understood on some level that even though our baby was fragile physically, she gave off a strong, pure light. Maybe they needed her energy or her vibrations from the spirit world. Somehow, there seemed to be a magnetic attraction because people we didn't know were always at her bedside. I felt like Emily was this little person drawing people to God in some way.

I witnessed Emily's ability to heal others soon after she came to earth. One day my mother came with me to see Emily in the hospital. Mom looked at her and said, "Now I know what Johnny looked like." Johnny was her stillborn son who was whisked away and buried without a ceremony. In the days when he was born, people believed it was too painful for a mother to even lay eyes on her stillborn child. Mom buried all her grief and never spoke about her baby. On the drive home from the hospital that day, my mother began to talk about the experience of losing the brother I never knew. For the first time ever, she talked and she cried—then she talked and cried—and then she talked and cried some more. It was such a beautiful thing! Finally, all the grief my mother carried for years and years was healed. And our little Emily was sent by God to be her healer. How powerful is that!

From time to time, the nurses would call to tell me Emily wasn't doing well. Strangely, I wouldn't get really upset. One time we thought Emily was going to die during a cardiac event. Her heart was beating so fast it seemed ready to jump out of her little chest. She was given some antidotes and rallied. That's what she would do, all the time. Just when we thought she was going to die, she'd rally and be better. I'd continually say to myself, "Well, you never know what God and Emily are doing today."

After five months of intense, holy time together, Emily left this world and made her way to heaven. In the beginning, I'd go to Communion and call upon Emily. I knew she was with God, so for me, the best way to get close to her was receiving the Eucharist. One time I felt this little brush on my cheek as I was sitting in the pew after Communion and just knew it was Emily. I loved feeling this connection to our baby! After Communion I always felt very light—like a happy heart.

Emily engineered the connections involved with the two children we adopted after her birth and death. I really think she found them for us. There were so many divine interventions with both adoptions that I really felt each time Emily and God were arranging things. The details of the many synchronistic meetings are too great to explain here, but I know in my heart that Emily handpicked these babies for us.

Emily also inspired me to become a parish nurse—for me it's not a job, it's a mission. I always know when Emily and God are sending people to me for a reason. It's always a little blessing for me, or them, or both. Somehow we connect and we help each other. Each time it's so awesome! There's an element of grace about it that always touches my heart.

For nineteen years, Emily and I have shared a bond of deep love, and I always feel her presence. I believe she is still helping others to heal. One of the nurses who took care of Emily confirmed my belief when she sent me this note: "I still always think about you and the time we had with Emily. Whenever we have a sick baby, I pray to Emily to come and help the family. I also ask her, 'If this baby is to die, please help this little one cross over to the light.'" It's such a powerful thing to know that my Emily is a healer for those babies and their families.

Our daughter's spirit is still very much with our family and all those whose lives she's touched. We each have our "Emily stories" that show she's still watching over us and sending her love. Every day I thank God for my gift of connection to Emily and all the people she brings into my life! Together we bring healing to many.

Questions to Ponder

The questions below are intended to help you discover the various aspects of your many-faceted soul purpose. I invite you to spend time meditating on each question and then write down the insights that flow into your mind. This exercise becomes much easier when you ask for guidance and inspiration from your soul, your guides and angels, and, of course, your spirit baby.

1) What can I learn from my journey through grief?

2) How can I grow spiritually from this?

3) How can my grief open my heart and bring me closer to my soul?

4) How can my grief experience open my mind and help me to learn new concepts about life in the physical world and life in the spiritual world?

5) How can I heal and become a more loving being?

6) How can I generate more love, compassion, and empathy in the world?

7) What are the gifts in this tragedy?

8) What is my emerging soul purpose?

♥   ♥   ♥

Summary for Chapter Ten

1) Finding the hidden gifts in grief and embracing them shifts the outcome of your process from coping to healing.

2) Viewing your loss with soul eyes is the key to finding the gifts in the tragedy of miscarriage or infant death.

3) Perspective shifting is seeing with love, rather than viewing a situation through the eyes of fear.

4) Shifting to the new perspective is finding the blessing in the experience and using it to grow.

5) Soul growth and perspective shifting are different words for the same thing.

6) Perspective shifting allows healing to occur.

7) Soul growth is not automatic—it depends on the choices people make.

8) Dealing with the death of a baby often becomes the catalyst for transformation.

9) After the loss of an infant, many feel called first to heal their own grief, and then to take what they have learned and use it to discover their destiny—also known as a soul mission.

10) Often, but not always, this mission includes a burning desire to assist others who are healing after a grief experience.

Part III
Grief—The Doorway
to Spiritual Awakening

In this section of *Connected for All Time: Book One*, three heart-warming stories illustrate that what began as a terrible tragedy—a baby's death—is meant to be the crucible for a joyous spiritual awakening. As these three mothers move along their distinctive pathways for healing, they find the wondrous gift of connecting to Spirit. This awakening is the most important event in our soul journey here on earth. These inspirational stories—each one unique—contain profound wisdom.

CHAPTER ELEVEN

My Spirit Baby
Flutters Around Me

Knowing the spirit of my miscarried baby is around
makes me feel protected—like I have a special angel.
—Lynn, Devon's Mother

With long dark hair, bright sparkling eyes, and a radiant smile, Lynn is vivacious, attractive, and looks much younger than her fifty years. Born in the Midwest, she integrates small-town values into her daily life. And with an open heart, she quietly takes in everything until she has something to share. Then Lynn speaks with confidence and a quiet enthusiasm. She has answered the spiritual question, "Why am I here?" Lynn says with great passion, "I came to be the mother!"

Lynn finds motherhood very fulfilling; she gets great joy from sharing time with her children and guiding their growth. Once her three biological children were enrolled in school, Lynn and her second husband, Mario, opened their hearts and their home to their first foster child. Over the next six years, they were foster parents for a teenage boy and three babies, and then chose to adopt Jamie, the last baby who came to them.

During this time, Lynn's passion for mothering took a new direction when she began training other parents in foster care. These classes evolved into parenting workshops, which she now teaches around the country. Lynn actually glows when she talks about presenting her work to hundreds of these parents at national conferences. She also inspires parents doing foster care with the book she wrote, which she calls her pride and joy. It's quite evident that helping children by educating their foster parents is also a big part of her soul work.

Lynn has always had a very curious mind. At nineteen, she went exploring in a spiritual bookstore, where she picked up Edgar Cayce's autobiography, *There Is a River: The Story of Edgar Cayce*. Known as the sleeping prophet, Cayce was the most famous psychic of the last century. Reading this book was a transformational experience for Lynn; it opened her mind to the possibility of life after death and spirit communication.

As part of her spiritual development, Lynn scheduled an appointment with a spiritual medium, and was excited to move beyond reading books by having a personal experience. She spent weeks preparing for her session—even praying for three specific loved ones to come and communicate with her. Much to her surprise, Spirit had a different agenda!

Lynn's Reading

Below is a transcript of an intriguing portion of Lynn's session with the medium.

Medium: *Did you lose a child? A male child?*

Lynn: *I miscarried a baby, but it was too early to tell boy or girl.*

Medium: *I see you don't know—but I know. It's a he, not a she. I know because he is here, and he's telling me. On the other side he calls himself Devon. [Laughing] He's funny. He's laughing as he says in a singsong way, "My name is Devon. It rhymes with heaven. That's where we all go!"*

Lynn: *[Laughing]*

Medium: *He's standing behind you and talking to me. He's interesting because he's very analytical. He's telling me these messages to give to you. He thought it was an honor to be with you. He felt very safe with you. He felt very secure with you. It was the perfect place for him to be. To have experienced your motherly love—that unconditional love—for one moment, meant everything to him. It was worth it. It was very worth it! He would do it all again.*

[Laughing] If he had been born, he would have been the wild child—you know, pierced his ears and such things as that. He thinks that is very funny.

It caused great sadness within you when he left. He wants to acknowledge that. He keeps saying, "Don't cry, Mommy. Don't cry, Mommy. Don't cry, Mommy."

Lynn: *[Crying] I'm so touched.*

Medium: *You gave birth right after him? Or another child came to you inadvertently? Like maybe this one came another way? He's showing me somebody else holds the baby first.*

158

Lynn: *Yes, both are true. I gave birth to our son Matthew one year after the miscarriage. Ten years later, Jamie came to us as a foster child, when he was only eleven months old.*

Medium: *Devon was very close to this other son you had. He was very, very close. Their plan was to surprise you with another baby right away. He's explaining this to me saying, "Surprise!" He's laughing as he tells me this. One after another—that was the surprise.*

Lynn: *[Crying and laughing at the same time]*

Medium: *He's still standing right behind you. Now he looks like a little kid. Aww. He wants to make sure you're not mad. He says, "Don't be mad at us." And I'm telling him that, of course, you're not mad. He says, "I loved her mostest of all!"*

Lynn: *[Crying] Oh, my!*

Medium: *You guys gathered together prior to coming. All five of your children were there with you. They all decided they wanted you to be their mommy. You were selected by all of them.*

Lynn: *Really?*

Medium: *Yes. Devon says, "You picked me, and I picked you." You and Devon knew this was going to be a risk. You knew this miscarriage was to come. He says, "My mommy told me she would always love me no matter what. And no matter what happened, we would get through it together." He is acknowledging that.*

Lynn: *I don't remember saying that.*

Medium: *No, you wouldn't. That was your higher self—before you came to earth.*

Lynn: *Oh, I see.*

Medium: *Little Devon likes to shake things. He likes to shake trees and plants. He also likes to flutter. He lets you know that he's around by fluttering. So when you see a fluttering motion out of the corner of your eye, that's him. He's a flutterer!*

Lynn's Response to Her Reading

Lynn enjoys writing, so I invited her to put pen to paper and record her thoughts and feelings in response to this reading. One month later, she gave me this in-depth account of her experiences.

I believed these messages that came from my spirit son. However, I must say this all takes some getting used to; it's a different way of thinking. If somebody told me this story, I would say it was beyond belief. At the same time, I believe it because it was my experience.

It is hard to put into words how I felt when Devon showed up at my reading. I was hoping to hear from my cousin, who was like a sister to me, or my grandmother, or a mentor of mine who tragically crossed over from a brain tumor. All of these people come to me regularly in my dreams, and I was sure they would want to talk to me when I sat with a medium.

Instead, Devon, the baby I miscarried nineteen years ago, decided to come through with a loving message for me. Up until this session, I hadn't really dwelled on this miscarriage. Now, knowing the spirit of my miscarried baby is around makes me feel protected—like I have a special angel.

The whole miscarriage experience was rather bizarre. I had a viral flu and when I started bleeding, the doctors put me in the hospital at four o'clock in the afternoon to run all sorts of tests. We were not trying to have another child, so I was very surprised when they told me I was three weeks pregnant. I immediately put my hands over my uterus and began saying to my baby, "Hang on and it will be all right; just hang in there."

I was so happy to be pregnant! I remember praying to God to keep the baby safe inside me, but as morning came, the doctors said my hormone levels were dropping. I knew it was futile; the baby was leaving me, and there was nothing I could do about it. At the time, I cried a bit, mourning the loss of this baby. However, I have to admit there was not much of a bond with a baby that entered my world and exited in less than a day.

At the time of the miscarriage, I really didn't think about the soul of the child I lost; I was more concerned about recovering and getting pregnant again. That was one thing Devon did for me. We had two little girls at this point, and I wasn't sure if I wanted another child. Afterwards, the desire to get pregnant was very strong, and I did—just a few months later.

Since my reading, I think about Devon frequently. The medium told me that Devon is always near, and if I see a flutter, that's him. For years, I've seen movement out of the corner of my eye, but have never been able to pinpoint the source. It would happen at random moments several times a week or so. I was never scared, just frustrated because when I turned my head to see what was creating the movement, it was gone.

Now I know that the fluttering has been Devon all along. There is a certain strange quality of comfort that I derive from knowing this. It takes a bit of getting used to, but I feel as if I have all my children with me now—even though Devon is just a flutter in a passing moment.

My husband, Mario, has a habit of staying up late at night after everyone has gone to bed. One night he heard little kid footsteps running through the downstairs of our two-story home. Thinking Jamie was out of bed, he got up to discipline him and send him back upstairs. To his surprise, there was no Jamie. Everyone was fast asleep! Mario was mystified about these footsteps. It's happened twice now. It isn't scary, just intriguing. Since the medium told us about Devon, Mario and I think this must be Devon's little spirit running through the house. It's a fun thing to think about!

I feel extremely lucky to have learned about the baby I never knew. No, I can't hold him in my arms and smell his skin, but I can take his words of love into my heart and treasure the special gift I have received.

Because of my work with Dr. Wesch and my spiritual reading, I have added another child into my family. What could be more wonderful than that?

One Year Later

One year later, Lynn and I had a lengthy discussion about her spiritual development and the changes that she experienced during this time. Here is a transcript of part of our conversation. I asked Lynn, "Are you still noticing Devon as the flutterer?" She gave this very thoughtful answer.

Yes! After the medium's spiritual explanation, I seem to be aware of a lot more fluttering! There's no pattern to it; sometimes it's three to four times a day, and then maybe I won't notice it for a few days. I really am not sure if the fluttering is more frequent or I'm just noticing it more.

Also, in the past month I've seen more than just fluttering glimpses. I'll be sitting in bed, and I notice something (like a shadow) running past my bedroom doorway. Again, it's out of the corner of my eye, so by the time I look there's nothing really there. It's happened three or four times. I know it's Devon, so I call out to him, "Would you just slow down so I can see you?"

My heart feels warm and full of love knowing that Devon is a spirit who is beside me, or behind me, or fluttering around me. I don't question, "Is Devon here with me today?" I just know he is. Actually, I'm developing a relationship with his spirit; I think about him a few minutes every day, and I believe he often gives me little bits of inspiration.

Just knowing that he is always around fills in a hole—the hole I used to have in my heart from missing the baby I miscarried. After hearing from my spirit son, that hole just filled in with the knowing.

I get a kick out of sensing Devon fluttering. It's a feeling of connect-edness that is hard to put in words. I used to have this tenuous thread of a connection with Devon. Since my reading, the tenuous thread that I never noticed grew into a thick rope—and the love travels back and forth through the rope. I feel very lucky!

Two Years Later

Lynn's ability to connect with Devon seemed to keep expanding over time. Her father made his transition several years after Lynn's session with the medium. After his passing, there was a significant shift; Lynn's house seemed to be bursting with spiritual energy. Lynn, Mario, and Jamie all started seeing, hearing, and feeling such fascinating things!

Mario has started seeing this flash of movement around the house. It's always out of the corner of his eye—then it's gone when he really looks. Each time he tells me of another incident, I just smile and say, "Welcome to my world, sweetheart! That's our Devon saying hello."

Devon has become a little trickster. At first, I thought I was losing my mind. Things like my papers and keys just keep getting moved— they turn up in the weirdest places. One time my car keys were missing. I looked all over for hours. Finally, I gave up and got the second set from our hiding place. Then, as I picked up my purse, I saw my keys in plain sight lying right on top of everything. There was no way they could have stayed at the top when I was rifling through my purse earlier.

I laughed out loud and said, "Is that you Devon? What do you want? Oh, I get it! You just want me to acknowledge you. I know you're here, and I know you love us. We love you, too!"

I've had several very subtle experiences of something touching me. One night, as I was about to fall asleep, I felt someone pat me on the top of my head. It was such a loving touch! I looked and, of course, there was nobody else around. Another time I distinctly felt something brush against my bare leg. I looked down expecting to see one of our cats—they were nowhere close.

One night Mario and I were just going to bed when we heard this popping noise in the house. It sounded like somebody popped a balloon. It was really loud! We looked all over the house but could find nothing. We didn't smell anything, so we decided it was nothing serious, like a gas leak. Finally, we just went to bed.

Then the next night, the same thing happened at bedtime, only louder. This time the "pop!" seemed to come from under the nightstand beside our bed. Our cat jumped straight off the bed! I looked all around the bedroom and came up with nothing. Mario and I knew we weren't imagining this "pop!" because the cat reacted. Besides, how could we both imagine the same thing at the same time? Could this be Devon? Why is he doing this? This one is still a mystery.

Our adopted son has also had some fascinating spirit experiences. Jamie and I were home alone one evening. I was lying on my bed reading when my son called out to me, "Mom, there's a tornado in the hallway! Come see!"

I rushed out of my room and stood in the hallway, where I could see nothing. Jamie looked wide-eyed, so I knew he was seeing something. I calmly said to him, "Tell me what you see."

Jamie kept staring at the end of the hallway as he said, "It's the color of Ike. (That's our gray cat.) It's spinning like a tornado. It just moved through my room, and I followed it out here in the hall. It's gone now. Wow! This is so cool!"

I walked down to the end of the hallway, but I felt nothing and saw nothing. I was so mad to have missed it! Of course, I knew this was Devon's spirit being a trickster again. He's such a little imp!

Points to Ponder

This pregnancy is so brief that Lynn does not even know she has conceived. Yet, Devon comes back nineteen years later and surprises his mother by communicating through a spiritual medium. Clearly, Devon's consciousness lives! He is still very connected to his mother and has the ability to deliver his message of forever love. Surprisingly, this powerful spirit being even has personality! Devon presents himself as a playful trickster and sends the powerful medicine of laughter and joy to his mother.

Most people, even women who have experienced a miscarriage, haven't given much thought to these questions: *Does a miscarried baby have a spirit? Does that spirit continue to exist someplace in the universe? Does the soul love continue to exist between the spirit of the baby and the earthly family members? Is the spirit of the miscarried baby able to communicate with earthly family members? Is it possible to have an ongoing relationship with the spirit of a miscarried baby?* Devon shows us the answer to each of these questions is YES!

This story is a dramatic reminder that each unborn baby is actually a powerful soul with consciousness. It also reminds us that even the shortest of pregnancies has great significance at the spiritual level.

CHAPTER TWELVE

Spreading More Love
in the World

We sometimes need a nudge to practice loving our fellow beings.
People respond with open hearts
when you ask in the name of an angel baby.
—*Kacie, Chandler's Mother*

Kacie is a resilient young woman who, after her baby's death, was able to use this tragedy as the crucible for her own joyous spiritual transformation. As you will see, she healed her soul wound in a few short years. Here is her remarkable story as she told it to me.

Out of the Darkness

I was only eighteen when my first baby, Chandler, died before being born. During the first ultrasound he was diagnosed with anencephaly (lack of brain development), and he died in the womb in the twenty-third week. This disease is always fatal; some die early in the pregnancy, some at birth, and some live a few days. In the beginning, I was lost in my grief with no hope of feeling peace or joy ever again. Gradually, with Chandler's assistance, I found my way out of the darkness. I love sharing the story of our healing journey.

Chandler Sends Comforting Lyrics

When Chandler first crossed over, I would often hear the song "Arms Wide Open" by Creed; it became our song. Here's a meaningful portion of the lyrics:

> *Welcome to this place.*
> *I'll show you everything*
> *With arms wide open.*
> *Now everything has changed.*
> *I'll show you love,*
> *I'll show you everything*
> *With arms wide open.*

Whenever I heard our song on the radio, I felt like Chandler was sending me a message, saying that when I see him again his arms will be wide open. It was always very comforting to imagine our meeting someday in heaven.

Another song also seemed to be a message from my spirit baby. Celine Dion sings a song entitled "My Heart Will Go On." In the early months of my grief, this song often played on the radio while I was driving. It reminded me then—as it does now—that Chandler's spirit is still with me and our love does go on.

These two songs seemed to come to me whenever I was down and needed some encouragement. I knew this was Chandler's spirit watching over me and making sure I heard these comforting lyrics when I needed to be cheered up.

My Healing Journey

I was raised to believe in angels and in life after death. However, when Chandler died, these convictions brought me no comfort at all. My beliefs crumbled and I turned my back on God. My heartache, grief, hurt, and despair overwhelmed me. Being only eighteen, I just didn't know how to handle losing my precious baby. For the first few years, I was stuck in so much grief that I isolated myself, crying my heart out. I cried for hours with no relief, yet couldn't seem to stop, so I decided to see a therapist. One day he asked, "Why do you feel you need to keep crying so much?" I answered, "The more I cry, the more I show Chandler how much I love him. Stopping would mean I'm disloyal to his memory."

My therapist gave me some great words of wisdom that changed my whole outlook about continuing to suffer. He said, "You already know that thoughts and feelings are energy. Your crying and suffering is sending negative energy to Chandler. Do you really want to continue doing that? Let's think about how you could send positive energy to him."

It was such an "Aha!" moment—I had angel bumps everywhere! Right then I made a choice to stop crying. It was like flipping a switch. I took hold of myself and started sending Chandler smiles and messages of love instead of my usual sad thoughts. This was quite easy once the decision was made. I simply shifted my focus to happier things I could do. It worked! My whole world began to change once I made this choice, and I felt inspired to create many positive things in my life.

Spreading More Love in the World

Together Chandler and I have a goal to spread more love in the world. Since his transition, I've created many positive things in my life. I consider them all gifts from Chandler. Without him, I never would have been motivated to create these projects.

The Memorial Garden

About four years after Chandler's passing, I created a memorial garden for him. It's filled with my favorite flowers and has a few places where I can sit quietly and meditate. Even now, years later, I often take my journal with me and sit amidst the beauty. I write letters to Chandler, telling him about my new spiritual awakenings and all my happy moments—it's easy to stay away from anything sad.

Sometimes I ask the angels to talk to me, and then I write whatever comes into my mind—this is called automatic writing. Their messages are things like: "Chandler is safe. He still loves you. He's around you every day." The messages that flow through me are quite comforting.

I now give workshops and teach others how to create their own gardens to honor a deceased loved one. Leading these workshops is one of my greatest joys in life.

Random Acts of Kindness

Chandler inspired me to design a website in his memory and invite communication from other families who had babies with anencephaly. In a short time, we had almost four thousand hits on this website. I'm thrilled so many people are getting support and information.

One day, I felt inspired to place this notice on the website: "Please do random acts of kindness in memory of Chandler. Then send me an e-mail describing them. I'll keep them in Chandler's memory book." I asked my friends and family to do the same. My heart glows reading the responses from everyone, and I'm so grateful to have played a tiny part in it. After all, this is my way of helping Chandler spread more love in the world.

It seems we sometimes need a nudge to practice loving our fellow beings— and people respond with open hearts and a desire to help when you ask in the name of an angel baby. Babies open hearts without prompting. They touch people in ways that are magical, and folks really like to help out when babies are involved.

Creating an On-Line Support Group

Another friend and I created an on-line support group for parents who had lost babies to anencephaly. This project grew out of our website. In just the first two months, we connected with eight members who live all over the world. We think this was just an awesome beginning. Who knows how big it will grow!

My friend and I teach the parents who come to our website various ways to remember their babies in a positive light. It's so inspiring for us to give them ideas and watch their lives change over time. When they first contact us, most mothers are very stuck—they're in a hole and don't know how to get out. All they need is encouragement and some coaching; then they start moving. One mother wrote me, saying, "Thank you! God bless your work! Your ideas have brought our whole family together." I know Chandler is with me and is also guiding me to help all these families.

Many of the mothers I work with are wondering if the spirit of their baby is upset with them. They carry so much guilt about their infants having this disease. I believe Chandler inspired me to give them this message:

> *Your baby chose this path. Your baby chose you as a mother because you have a beautiful heart and a great ability to love. This soul knew you would give enough love so he or she could go to the next spiritual level. You did the most important job a mother could do—you helped the spirit of your baby advance.*

These words from Chandler seem to bring great consolation to these grieving mothers. As they embrace this spiritual viewpoint, their guilt seems to vanish. It's so rewarding to deliver my son's words of wisdom and help these mothers heal.

Hospice Work

Five years after Chandler's transition, I felt an urge to become a hospice volunteer. My grandmother received hospice care, and I never forgot how blessed we felt with the volunteers who came to be with her. At first I was afraid I couldn't do it, but I just love it. My happiest days are the days I do this sacred work.

Chandler was definitely with me throughout my training. Here's my journal entry on graduation day.

> *Today I graduated from my hospice-training program. We took a tour of a nearby mortuary. The mortuary was beautiful and so very*

peaceful. Finally, we saw the urn viewing room. I was awed by how gorgeous some of them were, like china vases. The baby urns really struck a chord with me. They had a beautiful one that I would have loved to purchase when Chandler was cremated. It showed an angel on a cloud. They also had a really sweet pendant for wearing some of the ashes.

The second I got in my car and shut the door, the floodgates opened, and I cried and cried. I was just wishing that when my son passed away I had been able to think more clearly and had not been so rushed. I would have chosen an urn like the angel one or maybe had a little service.

I turned on the radio and the song "My Immortal" by Evanescence had just started playing. I instantly knew that it was a sign that Chandler was with me at that very moment, and that he was drying the tears that spilled from my eyes.

So far, I've visited four different people with my hospice work. I never intended to bring up Chandler, but people always ask if I have children. I gingerly told one lady about losing my son, and this opened the door for her to talk about the baby she'd lost. Then I told a woman in her sixties about Chandler. She opened up and began to talk about her daughter who had lost three babies—two SIDS deaths and another with Down's Syndrome. There are no accidents! Can you imagine? These women are having healings on their deathbeds! What a blessing! It was really meant to be that I was assigned to them.

I can feel Chandler glowing with pride as we work together providing hospice care. I would never have volunteered for this work if Chandler hadn't died as an infant. I believe my son helps the office workers choose the patients they assign to me for the specific purpose of connecting and sharing our story. It's a powerful story filled with inspiring moments and deep lessons about the value of looking for the joy!

The Best Gift Ever

Six years after Chandler's transition, I decided to take a class on angel communication. My teacher, Sunny, also talked about recognizing signs and receiving messages from deceased loved ones. When I heard this, I knew I had been missing a lot of signs from Chandler. Of course, I was guided to find this angel class—there are no accidents! It was exactly what I needed to take the next step on my healing journey, because after this course everything opened up really wide. It was fantastic!

Immediately after my class, I received the best gift ever from Spirit. I came out of my bedroom and actually saw Chandler running towards me in the upstairs hallway. The vision was just as clear as it could be. He looked about five years old with brown hair, and he was wearing jeans, a red shirt, and cute little tennis shoes. My son was smiling and running towards me with his arms wide open—like he was coming to give me a great big hug. It was a moment of creating heaven on earth—I saw him with arms wide open, just like he promised, and I didn't have to die before this could happen. It was over in a flash; he was there, and then he vanished. I was blown away! Never in my wildest dreams did I expect such a thing to happen.

Chandler blessed me with this visit, and since then nothing's been the same! I have absolutely come to joy about my relationship with him! Now that I'm happy, I can see and feel his happiness. When I was so miserable, I would never have appreciated or wanted to see how joyful and fulfilled Chandler was in Spirit—my missing him and the pain I felt were too overwhelming for that. Now, when I think of him, it's like a sunny day, and everything is bathed in light! This visitation was pivotal for me! We have a theme—we love each other with our hearts and arms wide open.

Visitation Dreams

After I had this vision, Chandler started coming into my dreams quite regularly. Many mornings I would wake up with such a joyful feeling, and then remember I'd just had another visit from him. In the dreams, Chandler is still a baby, and I'm just doing regular everyday kinds of things with him—like playing in the park, walking through the grocery store, or taking him to the zoo. We seem to be doing all the things I never really got to do with him when he was here. I'm always holding him, and often the people we meet say things like, "He's so cute!"

These dreams have been very nurturing for me. My heart longed for the chance to do all the typical "mommy things" with Chandler, and so I guess we're doing them together while I sleep. And what mom doesn't want everyone to admire and adore her beautiful baby? Well, that is my experience in the dreams, and I love every compliment and every adoring glance. I feel like a real mom in those moments.

Sometimes, I had my doubts about whether the dreams really meant my son was coming to visit me. I wondered if I was just making it up, because I wanted it so much. My doubts were relieved in a very surprising way. I attended a book signing with Lynn Bunch, author of *Stepping Beyond Judgment*. As Lynn signed my book, she asked me to wait and meet with her when she was finished. When we were alone, she said, "I need you to hold my hands. Your son wants you to feel him for the first time. Feel the energy coming through my hands? Your son is sending that energy. He loves you, and he's around you all the time. He says to tell you, 'Mommy, come see me in your dreams again.'" I was thrilled to have the confirmation!

Chandler's dream visitations give me moments and memories that I will always treasure. It's so delightful to know they are real and not just wishful thinking. My spirit baby and I continue to bond in my dreams. I always awaken with such joy!

Chandler and Uriel Are With Me

In the angel class, I learned to use automatic writing to connect with angels, as well as my spirit baby. It's been a wonderful tool for getting messages from Chandler. I simply get quiet and ask him for inspiration; then I start writing ideas that come into my head. Each time I receive wonderful words of spiritual wisdom that help me continue to move forward on my healing journey.

After the angel class, I became very connected to Archangel Uriel. He's an archangel who carries a lantern to light our pathway here on earth. When I meditate, Uriel often brings me messages that tell me my emotions are healing.

Eight years after Chandler's death I drove up to Sedona, Arizona with my family. We took some time out while we were there to do some easy rock climbing and visit one of the vortexes—energy centers where the veil between the two worlds gets very thin. I thought maybe I could get a better connection to the spirit world in such a place. We made the easy climb to a plateau on the red rock mountain, where I took a few moments to sit quietly and take in all of the beauty.

I had just bought a picture of Uriel at a store in Sedona and felt guided to bring it with me to the vortex. Sitting in silence, I placed my hand over the picture and asked that Archangel Uriel bring me a message for my highest good. Then I wrote in my journal, putting down whatever came into my head. These beautiful, loving words came to me:

See yourself in me. Absorb me, angelic presence that you are. Inhale my light. You are love. Feel the ground and remember this: We are one. Chandler is with me and he loves you. He is wise. He is here. Look around and know that he is this—the beauty of the earth. You are love.

A Light in My Aura

Months later, I made a plan to return to Sedona to celebrate Chandler's birthday. I wanted to treat myself to a wonderful day of high energy and metaphysical fun. The week before, I had talked to Chandler and confided my plans to him, saying, "I'm going to have my aura picture taken on your birthday, and you'd better show up!" As I sat before the special aura camera, I deliberately didn't tell the photographer anything about Chandler.

When I looked at my aura picture, I was thrilled to see a bright light just above my left shoulder. The aura photographer was also a psychic and interpreted the picture saying, "This bright light is masculine energy; it's around you all the time." Then I told her about Chandler. Isn't it just too cool that I have a photo of Chandler—and on his birthday, no less!

I loved getting this physical proof of Chandler being so close to me. He's not out there in heaven somewhere; he's right here in my aura. No wonder I feel so close to him. This picture is worth more than a thousand words—it's absolutely priceless!

Miracles in My Life

Chandler and I have such a wonderful, positive relationship, and that is so much better than crying all over the place and being depressed and in pain. It's never too late to come to joy about your loved ones on the other side. You can learn to see the blessings that come because they were in your life and live on in your heart.

I know Chandler came to me because he saw the potential of what we could do together by connecting with love and compassion to so many others who need healing. My spirit son inspires me to discover various ways we can do this. I'm open to even more ways, and I'll put effort and love into every project he encourages me to start.

Our dear Chandler made his transition ten years ago. I look back at the young girl who gave birth to him, and I'm amazed at how much she's grown during this short time. Chandler has been the catalyst for all my spiritual growth. He opened the door, and I made a choice to walk through it. I've become an ordained minister, a certified spiritual counselor, and a volunteer at Hospice of Arizona.

With Chandler at my side, I now dedicate my time and energy to helping others in grief. My life is so rich and filled with so much love. It's a miracle!

I'm so very grateful to Chandler for inspiring this wealth of sacred work in my life. Together we are spreading more love in the world—and that's a miracle, too!

Points to Ponder

Kacie demonstrates that after the death of a beloved infant, it is indeed possible to put an end to grief and suffering and then consistently think of your baby with love instead of pain. The catalyst for this transformational healing is her therapist's suggestion that her suffering is sending negative energy to Chandler. This is the turning point for Kacie's journey through grief. After two years of crying, this courageous woman makes a choice to stop grieving and shifts her focus to creating positive things in the world. It is such an empowering choice! What a defining moment for Kacie! Throughout Kacie's healing journey, Chandler, her spirit baby, sends powerful medicine in the form of songs, inspiration, guidance, and pure love so she can achieve this transformational healing. Mother and son now share a deep soul love and have an ongoing, evolving relationship dedicated to generating more love on the planet.

My hope is that this story will inspire you and many others to heal. I invite you to share Kacie's story with anyone who may still be suffering after the loss of a beloved infant. As you do so, you will be joining Kacie and Chandler in spreading more love in the world. It's a very soulful thing to do!

CHAPTER THIRTEEN

Answering the Call of Spirit

The undeniable urge to write
about my healing journey was a spiritual calling.
The inspiration came from Miranda, my angels,
spirit guides, and deceased loved ones.
I was also called by God. It is a life purpose
I was born to fulfill.
—*Monica, Miranda's Mother*

Monica was vivacious, charming, and very thoughtful as she related this fascinating story of her thirteen-year healing journey. As you will see, she meandered down a spiritual path of connecting and disconnecting, remembering and forgetting, waking up and going back to sleep. It's my joy to share her journey of spiritual growth with you.

Unspeakable Sadness and Despair

When I was told Miranda had no heartbeat, shock washed over me. How could this have happened to me? My baby girl was due to be born in just two days. Suddenly, my entire belief system about life (bad things don't happen to good people) was proven wrong. The death of my baby filled me with unspeakable sadness and despair, and wrapped me in a thick layer of fear and vulnerability. If my baby could die, then so could my two-year-old daughter, Alex, and my husband, Al, and so could I. It brought the reality of death into the forefront of my consciousness.

The day I came home from the hospital without Miranda was one of the most painful days of my life. It was raining so hard it seemed like the very heavens were crying with me. After the heavy rain subsided, I walked outside by myself. The sun in the west was shining against a black eastern sky. As a few remaining drops of rain fell on my face, I wondered about my daughter and spoke to her in my mind. Can you see me or hear me? Do you know how much I love you and desperately miss you? I felt completely disconnected from her and prayed that she was now in a better place, peaceful and beautiful, surrounded by love. That was the only thought that made me feel even remotely better.

As I looked out toward the dark sky, a rainbow appeared, full and vibrant. I marveled at its beauty when suddenly a second rainbow emerged, just above the first one. I couldn't remember the last time I'd seen a double rainbow. My God, it was incredible! I was overcome by a warmth in my heart and the undeniable feeling that this was a sign meant for me, from God or perhaps from Miranda, telling me she was okay and that she was with me in spirit. It's what I wanted to believe. I watched and wondered until the rainbow faded away.

I would later learn that in Scandinavian mythology, the rainbow is thought to be a path to the gods along which the souls of children are called. I also discovered that many cultures believe the rainbow is a bridge between heaven and earth, often seen as a message of hope. I was uplifted for maybe a day with this sign from Miranda, but then my overwhelming grief returned full force. One rainbow wasn't enough to keep my deep sorrow at bay.

We shared our sad news with family and friends. We wanted the whole world to know our Miranda had been born in spite of the fact that we didn't get to bring her home. Even though most of my family and friends never got to hold her close or stroke her soft cheeks and dark hair, she had lived. And even though I would never get to rock her to sleep with a lullaby or nurse her at my breast, see her first steps, hear her first words, watch her grow up—I loved her as much as any parent loves a child. There will always be an empty place in my life where she should have been.

In the first weeks, I was overcome by feelings of isolation and was afraid to be home alone. I couldn't concentrate on anything. Even the simplest of things, like playing with my two-year-old, was a struggle. I lost interest in everything I had once enjoyed—music, reading, even television became repulsive. How could life go on around me when my whole world had fallen apart? I felt cheated, betrayed, angry, and jealous when I saw other people being happy, especially pregnant women or women with young children or babies.

For the first months, I didn't believe that I would ever be happy again. Yes, I had a loving husband and a wonderful daughter, but it wasn't enough. I wanted my baby girl back. I yearned to hold her and shower her with all the love that still filled my heart.

After Miranda's death, I noticed that most people didn't have a clue about what to say to me and often made upsetting comments. One well-meaning friend said, "At least you didn't know her." Well, let me tell you my answer to that!

I met my baby girl when I first heard her beating heart. Our relationship grew every time I felt a little thump that said, "Hello, Mommy." I sympathized with her when the hiccups seemed to go on for hours. Like any proud mother, I watched her and my belly grow, little by little, day by day. I knew what her name would be and imagined her brown hair, hazel eyes, and long eyelashes.

I knew the fun we'd have, the four of us walking hand in hand: one with mom, one with dad. "Table for four, please." Ballet classes and Girl Scout meetings. Catching frogs and fireflies. Snuggling in for bedtime stories, one on my left, one on my right. Baking cookies, daddy-daughter dances.

I knew the adventures our two siblings would have. Playing make-believe and hide-and-seek. Building sand castles and snow forts. "Wake up, wake up, Santa came!" Jumping in leaf piles and giggling under the covers. "Mom, she took the last cookie!" Whispering secret messages through the heat registers.

I also knew the dreams I had. Her first kiss, her first prom, her first heart-break. Football games and graduation, college dorms, wedding ceremony. Her first baby, my grandchild. I knew what could have been.

Beginning My Healing Journey

I was determined to move through my overwhelming grief, so I was quite proactive about healing right from the beginning. I did whatever I could to make that happen. Mostly I did things instinctively—things that made me feel good, like getting out of the house for lunch with a friend, or taking my daughter, Alex, to play with other children at the playground. I had to function because I had to be mother to our two-year-old.

My grief therapy was mainly talking about Miranda to whoever would listen. Family, close friends, neighbors, and even coworkers generously gave so much time and energy as they listened to my feelings and my many questions. I was so desperate for support that I just kept reaching out and talking to people. I called my cousin who had lost a baby a few years earlier. After sharing for hours on the phone, she referred me to several other grieving mothers. I called these women I didn't even know because it felt so wonderful to talk to others who were grieving the same loss.

Just three weeks after Miranda's passing, I joined an infant loss support group. Attending this monthly meeting was the most helpful thing I did for myself. It was really hard to be there because the meetings were so emotional and intense. However, right away, I saw the benefit of being in the same boat.

We were all asking the same questions. All of our lives had been blasted apart. We could scream, cry, or be pissed off and still be accepted. I certainly didn't feel people would accept these emotions anyplace else.

The best part of group was what I call the "Dawn factor." Dawn had been in the group a full year when I came in—she was grieving the loss of premature triplets. I would arrive at meetings, and she would be talking and laughing with some of the more experienced group members before we got started. Here she was laughing even though she had lost three babies! It gave me hope that I would also laugh again one day.

After I was in the group for three months or so, I would watch a new person come in. Then I could see how far I had come. This gave me confidence that I was truly healing. The old group members and the new ones both became a measuring stick for assessing my progress.

When I went back to work, three months after Miranda's passing, I formed a great bond with another woman who had also had a death in her family and was seeking spiritual answers for her grief. Over our lunch hours, we shared spiritual books and had long talks about life, death, life after death, and spirit communication. It was so uplifting to dialogue with another spiritual seeker. Our talks filled a big void; consequently, I found myself waiting eagerly for our next lunch hour discussion.

Before Miranda died, I had started to awaken spiritually. About two years before Miranda's passing, my mother, who is a very spiritual person, gave me *Embraced by the Light* by Betty Eadie as a Christmas gift. Reading this book about life and death touched my heart and prepared me somewhat for changing my thinking about our baby's death.

Six months after Miranda's passing, I was drawn to read the book again. This passage had a profound impact on my thinking about her short life:

> *I saw many spirits who would only come to the earth for a short time, living only hours or days after their birth. They were as excited as the others, knowing that they had a purpose to fulfill. I understood that their deaths had been appointed before their births—as were all of ours.*
>
> *These spirits did not need the development that would result from longer lives in mortality, and their deaths would provide challenges that would help their parents grow. The grief that comes here is intense, but short. After we are united again, all pain is washed away, and only the joy of our growth and togetherness is felt.*

After losing our daughter, these words made so much more sense and helped me believe there was meaning to her life. I finally began to understand that her short time with us had purpose, that there was a reason for her coming and leaving so soon. This new view of death brought so much comfort to my wounded heart.

Looking back, I see it was no accident that my mother gave me this book; rather, God, Spirit, the Universe, or however you want to say it, was actually preparing me—giving me an opportunity to explore this spiritual view about death. My mother was just the messenger! Now, I feel blessed to know that unseen forces were assisting me on my healing journey—at the time, of course, I had no clue.

Unexplainable Moments

I've always believed in life after death, the paranormal and spirit communication; in fact I've been fascinated with ghost stories since my childhood. So when Miranda died, I believed in the possibility of spirit communication, but had never experienced it myself. I desperately wanted Miranda to contact me; however, even after the double rainbow, I really didn't know what to expect. I found myself wondering, "How will I know when she's sending a sign? What if I miss it? Have I already missed some?" Then these "unexplainable moments" began happening to me; this one very special moment got my attention.

A White, Flying Fluffy

About a month after Miranda's death, Al and I took Alex, who was still two, to an outdoor concert. We were lazing on the grass waiting for the music to begin, and I was daydreaming of how I should be holding Miranda and nursing her. She was often in my thoughts; I was peaceful, yet very sad. I looked up and saw a white, flying fluffy above my head. It was a seed from a cottonwood tree, and it was idly hovering over me. I reached my hand up, and it kept floating all around my hand. Despite a light breeze that should have blown it away, there it stayed, gently dancing around my hand for about two or three minutes! I could hardly believe it! My rational mind argued this couldn't be real—although I did recognize for a moment that something unusual was happening here. Hidden in my heart was the belief that this experience was very real, and deep down, I knew Miranda was showing me she was right there with me.

A Wind-Blown Ad

Five months later, I was looking for something, like a china doll, to put on the mantle, a representation to keep Miranda in my thoughts. I have a photograph of our daughter after she died, dressed in a lovely, soft gown that hospital volunteers made for that purpose, yet I was hesitant about putting it on the mantle. I thought other people would most likely be uncomfortable seeing a picture of our baby.

I found a porcelain angel in a catalog and ordered it. When it came, I placed it on the mantle, but the angel had blonde hair and blue eyes and didn't remind me of Miranda, so I sent it back. The same catalog then came out with another angel child that had brown hair, which excited me—so I ordered that one. I also ended up sending that one back because it just didn't fit—somehow it just wasn't what I wanted as a reminder of my little baby. Eventually I found an angel in another catalog, only this was a picture on a plate. The angel child was beautiful, with long, dark hair and a round face like Miranda's. While it seemed the perfect thing, I didn't do anything about it because I didn't want to be disappointed again.

Several weeks after seeing this ad, I was out for a walk when I spotted a piece of paper blowing around. I always pick up stray bits of garbage as I walk to keep the neighborhood looking neat and clean. I picked up the trash and couldn't believe my eyes. It was the very same ad for the angel plate I had been thinking of buying! I knew this was my own personal message telling me the plate was meant for me. So I ordered it.

When the plate arrived, I held my breath as I removed it from the package. I found myself looking at the most beautiful angel child wearing a white dress with pink highlights. The angel had long, dark eyelashes, and her head was bowed, so it looked as if her eyes are closed. Actually, she is looking down at a white bunny and holding a pink ribbon that is draped over the furry, little animal. What an interesting coincidence! My hospital picture of Miranda is almost identical! Her hand-made gown is soft pink with little white bunnies on it and has a pink and white ribbon too, and of course, her eyes are closed. I was inspired to get the plate for the very reason that everything is so similar—it does remind me of my picture of Miranda—and this plate doesn't make anyone uncomfortable; it makes them smile!

My Brain Vetoed My Heart

I didn't know how to explain these mysterious experiences of the white flying fluffy and the ad for the angel plate that blew across my path. Consequently,

I didn't even tell my friends or family for a long time. My reasoning was, "If you can't explain it, then don't talk about it." I was secretly hoping they were signs from my dear Miranda, but I didn't know this to be true. And I didn't want to look foolish by claiming something others might define as crazy thinking. Both of these experiences were so subtle—nothing like the dramatic scenes of spirit communication on TV. This made it even harder to hold on to the belief that it could be Miranda.

Looking back, it's pretty amazing to me all the ways I had for denying what I felt in my heart and thus shutting Spirit out of my life. When the ad blew into my path I actually laughed out loud. Again, I got this warm feeling in my heart and I felt such excitement. In the moment, my heart said, "This is a sign from Miranda!" However, within hours, my brain kicked in, and I explained the ad away as "just a coincidence." I consistently used that word to describe all the unexplainable things that kept happening around me.

Now it's obvious to me that these events were Spirit guided. Intuitively, I knew the truth right from the beginning, but my intuition was not strong enough to override my logical mind. So for years I allowed my brain to veto what my heart was saying.

Seeing Triple Numbers

Ever since Miranda died, I've had this fascinating thing going on with our digital clocks. When I look at the clock, the numbers are often all the same: 1:11, 2:22, 5:55, or 11:11. It began a few months after Miranda's passing and has continued now for thirteen years. It might happen two or three times a day, every day for a week, and then not again for a few months. It comes and goes. It's not that I sit and watch the clock all day. It often happens when I first walk into a room. Sometimes I'm awakened in the middle of the night with the urge to look at the clock, and I find the numbers are all the same.

At first, I didn't know how to interpret seeing triple numbers. A part of me wanted to deny this experience just like I denied all the other mysterious events. However, this was something I couldn't push under the rug because it happened so frequently. The repetition did not allow my usual denial mechanisms to work anymore. Within the first year, I decided this was something spiritual going on.

Now, after thirteen years, whenever I see the triple numbers, I feel this rush of excitement. It literally stops me in my tracks. I also find humor in it; I find myself laughing out loud every time it happens. I know seeing these numbers means something. Somehow, I'm guided to look at the clock at just the right moment. Recognition of this guidance tells me I'm not alone. It also gives me reassurance that someone's helping me and watching over me. Seeing triple numbers helps me feel joy, happiness, and wonder. To this day, I often wonder if it's Miranda, the angels, or other spirit beings giving me these little hellos—I always laugh and say hello in return. I don't really know, but I decided long ago that I don't have to know.

Another White, Flying Fluffy

After much reading about life after death and spirit communication, I had my first flying fluffy experience revisited in a big way! I was sitting at my kitchen table reminiscing about the mysterious flying fluffy experience at the concert eight years before. A huge rainstorm had just ended, everything was drenched and plastered to the ground; the trees were still dripping, and water was everywhere. The girls and I (since Miranda we had added two more daughters to our family) had errands to run, and we jumped at the chance to get them done before the rain started up again. We all went outside, and out of the blue, there was another one—another white flying fluffy came floating to me! I was really excited because it was the same kind from years ago. I showed the girls, who didn't quite get the significance but witnessed the rest of this interesting event. Here was a flying fluffy dry as can be, and not only was this white puff floating close to me, it began following me around! After a few moments, I decided to keep it, so I got a baggie and captured it.

I spent the rest of the day in a daze, trying hard to remember what had caused me to think about that first incident while I was sitting at the table that morning. By this time, I had enough information to know that Miranda was sending me another message, and at the same time, confirming my first experience as well.

Missing the Message

Three years ago (ten years after Miranda's death) I had my first interview with Dr. Wesch. I remember saying to her, "I've had just two or three experiences of spirit communication from Miranda." Then she explained all the different ways our deceased loved ones make their presence known. I was astounded! You could have knocked me over with a feather! Coming out of denial was like taking off blinders.

Dr. Wesch told me several stories of spirit babies sending their loved ones a message by making a musical toy begin to play. Another one of my unexplainable moments came to mind as she was talking.

About four years after Miranda's passing, I heard a musical toy playing in the downstairs playroom—and I was home alone. Then it happened again and again over the next several months; it always seemed totally random. Often this same toy would sound off when I walked through the playroom. Each time I wrote it off as "just a bad battery." I explained it away using logic because I've always had this analytical mind.

After hearing Dr. Wesch's stories, it occurred to me that I was ignoring messages from Miranda when they were right in front of me. My mind opened to a whole new perspective about my spirit daughter. Suddenly I could see and acknowledge that Miranda is all around me and always has been. With each contact, I believe she is trying to tell me, "I'm here. I'm alive and well and constantly offering you inspiration and guidance. I'm a powerful spirit guiding your life. You are never alone."

Hey, Mom!

Walking through the kitchen one day, I heard somebody whisper, "Mom." At first, I thought it was one of my three living children, but then I realized they were all upstairs involved in other things. It was loud and clear—just like a human voice. Feeling stunned and weak in the knees, I sat down in the family room as I tried to figure out what was going on. It happened so quickly and it was so subtle I doubted that I heard it. My thoughts raced. Did I really hear someone say, "Mom?" Who is calling me? Could it be Miranda? Could this be real? Maybe I just imagined it.

This whispered message happened about eight years after Miranda's passing. At the time, I didn't have enough information about spirit communication to know that a spirit can actually whisper, so I didn't let myself believe it was Miranda.

When I told Dr. Wesch this story, she assured me, "That was Miranda! Spirits do indeed have the ability to speak to their loved ones in a human voice. It's rare, but it does happen." Then she recommended I have a reading with a spiritual medium. This very gifted woman said, "Miranda is pointing to your ear. She's telling me she tries to whisper in your ear. Do you ever hear her?"

It took the information from Dr. Wesch and this confirmation from the medium for me to believe it was really Miranda calling to me that day. Without their guidance, I didn't know how to interpret a whisper that I wasn't even sure I heard. I needed validation to trust this almost imperceptible communication.

It's so amazing to believe! I feel special knowing that my spirit daughter would take the time and energy to reach out to me. It makes our connection even more precious. It was just a regular day, and she was right there with me!

Focus of Attention

In the first year after Miranda's transition, I noticed numerous unusual happenings. I knew Miranda had sent me a double rainbow, but I didn't know what to believe about the others: a white flying fluffy that danced around my head, an advertisement for an angel picture, and guidance to notice duplicate numbers on the digital clock. Then, for several years, without realizing it, I shifted my focus to my life and my living children and tuned out the spirit world—the signs faded away except for the triple numbers. Now I've come full circle and set my intention to be aware and pay attention to the spirit world, so I'm noticing signs more often again. *It's all about where you put your focus!*

After thirteen years of reading and learning about spirit communication, I no longer use logic to deny the many unexplainable moments that continue to appear in my daily life. Whenever I notice another subtle sign, I light up and think, "Oh, yeah!" I get a little rush of emotion, like when the phone rings, and it's a friend you haven't heard from in a long time. Each time I recognize another message from my spirit daughter, it's much like bumping into an old friend—it turns on my heart light. I love feeling our connection!

The Call of Spirit

About two years after Miranda's death, I was awakened out of a sound sleep in the middle of the night. I had this intense feeling that I needed to write down all the details of my experience with Miranda; somebody was telling me that it was important that I remember, but I didn't yet know why. So there I was scribbling on a yellow note pad while my family slept peacefully. Memories flooded in so fast it was almost impossible to keep up.

I recorded some of the scenes from my journey with Miranda, writing down every little detail I could remember—my motherly connection to Miranda while she was in my womb, hearing the news that our baby had no heartbeat, what people said and did in the hospital, seeing the double rainbow the day I came home without our baby, going to my first infant loss support group session, and the conversations with the people I met at

Chapter Thirteen: Answering the Call of Spirit

the group. Two hours later, the intense energy flow abruptly subsided and I went back to bed exhausted.

Strangely, I didn't touch that yellow pad for over a year. During that time, I had a feeling I was supposed to write, but the topic for a book was never clear to me. Should I write about my childhood, my kids, my beloved grandfather who had lived a rich and interesting life, or Miranda? Nothing ever felt right. Now, despite this middle-of-the-night inspiration, my many doubts seemed to inhibit me. "I have no writing degree. Who's going to want to read what I write? I have nothing important to say." All my negative thoughts kept me stuck in fear and indecision. I was essentially paralyzed.

Then, a very interesting event unfolded. I was driving home alone late on a Friday night after visiting my parents. Halfway there I got this urge to search for something interesting on talk radio. Typically, I would be listening to music at this time of night, but there I was flipping stations in search of talk radio. Within minutes, a woman's voice caught my attention and I perked up as I heard her say, "I'm an author, and my mission is to encourage new writers. You are an expert on your own life. Start writing that book you have inside of you. You have nothing to lose."

I sat in my driveway totally mesmerized while listening to this stranger for an entire hour. She seemed to be speaking directly to me and I didn't want to miss even one word. In the moment, I was aware this was no accident. Something led me to that radio show. What are the odds of finding a midnight broadcast from clear across the country that had a special message for me? I felt very blessed to know Spirit was at work in my life! It was exciting to feel led—and it was a direction that I had never before considered.

After this dramatic experience, there was no way I could ignore the call of Spirit. I began writing my story of hope and healing after giving birth to a stillborn baby girl. From the beginning it was clear to me this project was about sharing my story to help others. Some initial research showed there were currently only a few books written by a mother after the death of an infant. I knew others could use my personal story to find hope and to heal. This need inspired me to keep showing up day after day at my computer.

I initially started writing just about my own experiences. Then, it gradually dawned on me that most of my healing took place in an infant support group with six other women. They had become part of my story—we were all intertwined. Eventually, Spirit guided me to a totally new place—writing a book about the deep love shared in this group of seven women as we all helped each other to heal. This title was given to me one day: *The Good Grief Club*. It was perfect! (www.thegoodgriefclub.com)

The undeniable urge to write about my healing journey was a spiritual calling. The inspiration came from Miranda, the angels, my spirit guides, my deceased loved ones. I was also called by God. It is a life purpose I was born to fulfill.

Before starting to write each day, I created sacred space by lighting a candle, playing spiritual music, placing Miranda's picture on my desk, and asking for assistance from Spirit. I was very aware each time I sat at the computer that I was doing this project with a spiritual team. I made writing my spiritual practice.

I loved this exciting, creative process. It was so exhilarating to have an idea pop into my awareness and then find the words flowing in to express it in detail. It was like I was being given the words. To me, it was a sacred process. When writing, I always felt my connection to Spirit. Actually, I knew I might as well stop whenever I felt disconnected.

Writing the book has been very fulfilling for me. I'm a stay-at-home mom, so I'm often questioning my purpose. The book has given me a big sense of purpose, and I know without a doubt it's a big part of my soul purpose. Writing the book helped keep Miranda at the forefront of both my heart and mind—it was how I connected with my spirit daughter. I know she wouldn't feel so tangible if I hadn't done this project.

The writing process came very easily, and I believe it's because something unseen was there guiding the work. Spirit is so ethereal it's hard to know exactly who was sending the guidance. I suspect it was mostly Miranda, but I didn't hear a voice or see anything. Also, it could have been my angels, guides, and loved ones on the other side.

I was very aware that I wasn't writing this book alone. When I got stuck, all I had to do was ask for help—usually the answer came within twelve hours. There were days when I thought, "I'm not sure what to do here." Then an inspired thought would come to me out of the blue. Many times the ideas were coming so fast that I had to run dripping wet out of the shower to write them on the pad placed there for just that purpose. Other times while driving, I'd have to pull over to record the inspiration I was receiving.

I believe I was connected to many spirits while writing the book— Miranda, angels, spirit guides, and my Nana and Papa. I believe they all worked together, blending their energies to send inspiration to me. When an inspired idea came into my mind, I didn't try to figure out which one of my many helpers was responsible for it. That would have been very distracting. It simply didn't matter to me who was providing the assistance. I just took the idea and felt the glow in my heart! It was more proof that I was not alone. It was very comforting to know I was so connected.

Now that I've finished the book, I still feel connected to all the same spirits. They are still close, sending guidance and inspiration for my everyday life. I feel their presence and receive their signs in very subtle ways—like when I see the number patterns on the clock, or synchronistic experience happens, or something flows easily without much effort on my part, or I feel a sudden burst of joy for no apparent reason.

Gifts From Miranda

Now that time has given me a different perspective on losing our daughter, I can look back at my own life and see the gifts that Miranda brought to me. I was able to articulate these gifts in a presentation I gave at a memorial service for infant loss several years after Miranda's death, which I also included in my book, *The Good Grief Club*.

In *The Gift*, Danielle Steele wrote:

> *It's like some people just come through our lives to bring us something, a gift, a blessing, a lesson we need to learn, and that's why they're here. She taught you something, I'll bet...about love, and giving, and caring so much about someone...that was her gift to you. She taught you all that, and then she left. Maybe she just didn't need to stay longer than that. She gave you a gift, and then she was free to move on...she was a special soul...you'll have that gift forever.*

I'd like to share with you some gifts that Miranda has given me. She gave me the gift of growth. How do I know I've grown? I no longer get bent out of shape when a fast-food worker forgets to put the cheese on my cheeseburger.

Miranda taught me to try to live every moment to the fullest. It wasn't until she left her earthly body that I realized how precious human life is, and, as we're all too painfully aware, how short it can be. I may or may not have a future, and right here and now is all I'm guaranteed. I've learned to slow down, look into others' eyes and listen intently, taste my food, and notice the beauty and smell of each flower in my neighbor Alice's garden.

Miranda gave me the gift of compassion, encouraging me to reach out to others. Before I lost her, I was in my own little world with no understanding of pain and suffering. I've learned that almost every person I come into contact with has their own tragic story to tell, and as I pass people on the street or in a hallway, I wonder what sort of pain might lie under their polite smiles.

Miranda taught me about gratitude. After focusing for so long on what I didn't have, I finally realized I already had so much to be grateful for: my health, a family, a warm house on a cold winter night. I learned to appreciate the small things that add richness to life and make it worth living. A phone call from a friend just when you need it most. Laughter. Birds chirping. The smell of spring and new beginnings. Someone to hold hands with. The sun shining. Hearing the words "I love you."

She gave me the gift that keeps on giving, for I only need to think of her, and then my life—with all its trials and joys—is put into magnificent, crystal clear perspective. Miranda taught me not to fear death; to let go of my attachment to a physical body; that life continues and can be sweet again.

Despite the positive changes I can attribute to Miranda's existence, I concur with Rabbi Harold Kushner, who wrote in his book after the death of his fourteen-year-old son, "I am a more sensitive person, a more effective pastor, a more sympathetic counselor because of Aaron's life and death.... And I would give it up in a second if I could have my son back." I, too, would give it all up just to hold my child in my arms and have her smile up at me.

I still miss my baby's physical presence when I look for her with my human eyes; but when I use my soul eyes, I know her spirit is with me. I know—I must believe—she's safe, she feels my love, she urges me towards peace and joy, reminding me it was there all along in my heart, and that her life had purpose.

Final Steps of My Healing Journey

I've just turned forty and as I look back over my life I see how much I've changed since Miranda came to our family. My beautiful, precious baby who never took a breath or spoke a word has been the catalyst for me to grow and change many of my beliefs about life.

In my teens and twenties, I led what I now see as a rather shallow life. I was committed to completing my goals and getting ahead—like getting married and starting a family, which had great meaning for me. However, I would often "sweat the small stuff." Also, like other young people, I didn't give much thought to things like the meaning of life, and I certainly wasn't asking many deep questions. Before Miranda died, I felt I was living a charmed life and everything seemed to go my way. I thought this was my reward for being a good person. Of course, after Miranda, I had to reexamine this outdated, completely untrue idea.

Immediately after Miranda's death I felt lost and filled with despair, depression, fear, and helplessness. I found myself questioning, "Where is God in my life?" Now I see that, at that time, *I was very disconnected from Spirit.* Being in this state of disconnection—even though I was unconscious about it—was really quite painful.

I've had lots of friends my whole life, but this did not prevent me from *feeling very alone in my spiritual life.* In the early days, after my daughter's death, recognizing signs from Miranda didn't change my feeling alone because I didn't have a framework in which to hang these experiences. I'd have one of my unexplainable moments of spiritual connection, feel good for a while, begin to doubt, minimize it in my mind, and finally say, "It's nothing." During this time, I didn't even understand the significance of these early encounters with my spirit daughter.

Writing the book was the vehicle for me to move deeper and deeper into connection with Spirit—this includes Miranda. During the eight years of using writing as a spiritual practice, I gradually shifted from feeling alone and disconnected to feeling very connected to the merged energies of Miranda and others in the spirit world. At the same time, I learned to trust inspiration and the feelings in my heart instead of relying solely on my analytical abilities. In a nutshell, I moved from my head to my heart—a major change that I was not even intending or expecting.

So after years of vacillating between connection and disconnection, I have finally established a sustained relationship with Miranda and Spirit. Now, when I get quiet and open my heart, I can actually feel my connection to pure love from Miranda, my angels, my spirit guides, and my deceased loved ones. Inspiration comes flowing in from Miranda and Spirit whenever I ask for help about everyday situations or frustrations; then I'm lifted above my usual fears and doubts. I'd say I receive this kind of assistance several times a day. Because of Miranda, I know God is ever present in my life.

Another major change is the way I view Miranda. For the first years after her death, I thought of my daughter as a little baby. I spent hours holding her little baby things—it was my way of staying in touch with her. As a parent I'm dedicated to taking care of my children, so, of course, I had this deep desire to take care of Miranda though I felt helpless to do anything for her spirit. I didn't have a clue where to begin. This was one of the worst parts of my grief.

Now, as I'm completing my healing journey, I understand my daughter is a powerful soul who, for a very short time, took on the form of a baby to join our family. She was a powerful soul then, she is a powerful soul now, and she will be a powerful soul for all eternity. This major shift in perspective evolved very gradually during my many years of reading spiritual books, spending hours in meditation as I wrote my own book, and having ongoing, deep conversations with other spiritual seekers.

I must say viewing Miranda as a powerful soul has resulted in my greatest healing. This new view of my daughter helped me let go of my inner need to protect and take care of my little baby girl. As a powerful soul, Miranda no longer needs my protection or mothering. Knowing this helped me let go of so much pain. This was the final step in the journey of healing my deepest grief ever.

My relationship with my spirit baby keeps growing and changing, just as the relationships keep changing with my other daughters who are alive in the physical world. I believe I will always have a relationship with Miranda's spirit though it is very elusive and not at all concrete. I believe she's still alive and is part of our lives. In addition, she's responsible for looking out for my whole family—me, my husband, and our other three daughters. These are the beliefs that I take on faith even though there's no way of proving it to anyone who may question me.

The Coolest Show Ever

Months after completing the book, I was sitting on our covered deck on a hot summer afternoon watching the rain clouds gather. A white flying fluffy caught my attention as it fluttered a few yards in front of me. It was so light—like a feather floating along on the gentle summer breeze. My heart lit up with joy and excitement!

A light drizzle had started and I found myself thinking, "Wouldn't it be cool if another one flew through the yard." And it happened! A second cottonwood seed came fluttering along the same path as the first one, but strangely, the rain had no effect on it. Then a third came flying along even though the rain was now a heavy drizzle. Next, I could hardly believe my eyes! The rain became an all-out shower, but even so, a fourth white flying fluffy appeared and floated across my yard amidst the raindrops. I sat on my deck with my mouth wide open—it was the coolest show I've ever seen!

When something unusual like this happens, I know it's Miranda. This unexplainable moment was a confirmation that she is with me. To this day, I find myself totally amazed that my beloved daughter produced this show for me. In my heart I knew she was saying, "I'm always here, Mom. I hear your thoughts and prayers. All you have to do is ask, and I'll let you know I'm always close."

This show came at a time when I was having some anxiety about getting my book published. Incidentally, I spent eight years writing the book and then two years trying to get it published. As the months went on without finding a publisher, I found myself asking: "How is this going to happen? Am I doing the right thing? Am I alone in this? Do I still have guidance from Miranda and Spirit?" After this cool show of four white flying fluffies defying the laws of physics and magically moving through the rain, my thoughts changed to the following: "I am on the right path. Of course, I'm doing the right thing. I'm not alone in this. I'm very connected to Spirit. My life is being guided, and I trust that the right publisher will show up."

I love seeing this bigger picture of life. It's exciting and fulfilling to know I have a bigger purpose—that there's more to life than paying the bills and doing the laundry. Of course, I'm still learning, still seeking spiritual knowledge. Evolving is a life-long process. Occasionally, I still regress and forget, for a time, about my spiritual connection; during these times, I find myself feeling anxious, depressed, and struggling through life. Then I catch myself and shift my focus to my spiritual connection that is forever present and patiently awaiting my attention. Immediately, life begins to flow and my anxiety is replaced with a spiritual peace because I know I'm guided, supported, and protected.

All I need to do is remember who I really am. I am a powerful soul who is always connected to God, all the angels, my guides, my loved ones on the other side, and my precious baby, Miranda, who came to our family to awaken me to the truth of who I really am.

Points to Ponder

In this story, Monica describes her struggle to make sense of the many unexplainable moments that begin happening after Miranda's death. She vacillates for years between believing and not believing that her spirit daughter is making contact by sending subtle signs that are almost imperceptible. *Have you had your own unexplainable moments? Do you sense a warm feeling in your heart when you perceive a sign? Like Monica, are you using your logical mind to veto what your heart is telling you?* My hope is that this story will invite you to believe that, like Miranda, your spirit baby is always close by and patiently waiting for you to recognize the subtle signs and messages he or she is sending.

Monica creates her own healing journey by following the call of Spirit to write a book about her grief experience after Miranda is stillborn. This project takes ten years and becomes the driving force for Monica to move deeper into communion with not only her spirit daughter, but other spirits as well. Writing this book is of major importance in Monica's soul journey. In doing so, she finds the perfect path for healing her grief, mending her broken heart, and uplifting her spirit.

You also have your own perfect pathway for healing your grief after losing your beloved baby. This path is unique for each person, so don't assume you also need to begin writing. *Have you felt the call of Spirit? Do you have a passion building in your heart? Are you feeling inspired to do something different from what you've ever done before? Do you have ideas about being of service or giving back to the world?* Perhaps it's your spirit baby sending guidance and inspiration so you can begin your own unique healing journey. Like Monica, you can find your way by listening with your heart.

Evolving to higher and higher levels of consciousness is the most important soul growth anyone can accomplish. It is a universal purpose for every soul who comes to earth. Here we see Monica fulfills this purpose by making her writing a spiritual practice—as she writes, Monica is aware of constantly receiving guidance and inspiration from a spiritual team of unseen helpers. *Have you opened your mind to the possibility of shifting your consciousness? Have you changed your view of life, death, or the afterlife since the loss of your beloved infant? Do you have a spiritual practice? Have you connected with your own team of unseen spiritual helpers?*

Monica's path of spiritual evolution is not a direct route to enlightenment; rather, as you have witnessed, it is a very gradual meandering path of connecting and disconnecting, remembering and forgetting, waking up and going back to sleep. In the end, she achieves this important shift in consciousness: "Miranda is a powerful soul who only came in the form of a helpless little baby. She came to our family to awaken me to the truth of who I really am. I've come to understand that, like Miranda, I, too, am a powerful soul." *Can you embrace the idea that your spirit baby is a powerful soul who came to awaken you to the truth of who you really are? Do you know that you, too, are a powerful soul?* Yes, let me assure you, that is your true identity.

CHAPTER FOURTEEN

Conclusion

This book gives voice to the tiniest of unheard voices—the spirits of infants who have transitioned due to miscarriage, stillbirth, and newborn death. From beginning to end, this book has been orchestrated by the spirit babies. Essentially, they have taken the role of my muse throughout this writing journey that has taken ten years. Initially, I was unaware of their presence. Then sometime within the first year, Barbara Norman, a spiritual medium from Minneapolis, gave me this message.

> *The spirits of the babies in the stories have formed a collective and are working behind the scenes to help you. They are guiding the book as you write at your computer. They will bring more stories to you. This book is very important. They want this message out to the world.*

I felt the chills of confirmation as I heard these words. In fact, my whole body was awash with angel bumps. There was no doubting the truth of these statements.

I believe the spirit babies arranged the many miraculous, synchronistic meetings that brought each story to the book—including the wondrous meeting with Wachan, the Inca medicine man. I imagine the spirit babies pulling invisible strings and positioning this sacred man and all the mothers, fathers, siblings, and grandparents to cross my path. Spirit gave me a subtle signal during each synchronistic meeting so I wouldn't miss the gifts the spirit babies were bringing to me. Each time, a little zing of energy would light up my heart as a grieving loved one began to share experiences of spirit communication from a beloved infant. Then I would know, "Pay attention! Here's another story for the book!"

With these stories of deep healing and connection, the spirit babies have also invited you, the reader, on a journey of spiritual awakening. Imagine the spirit of your infant joining the collective of spirit babies attached to this book. Ask this powerful group of souls to guide you as you move along your unique path of healing your heart and reclaiming the lost pieces

193

of your soul. I wish you many blessings on your journey. May you find the "peace that passes all understanding." May the light of your soul once again shine forth through your eyes.

Acknowledgements

There are so many who have gifted me with their inspiration, guidance, and support so this book could become a reality. First, I'd like to acknowledge the assistance from Spirit: all the spirits of the babies in this book, as well as my own guides and angels, who worked with me from beginning to end. Throughout the writing journey I felt as if I had a "baby on my shoulder" giving me inspiration and guidance. Second, I'd like to thank all the mothers, fathers, siblings, aunts, and grandparents who had the courage to share their precious stories of communication from a beloved spirit baby. Their stories are the heart of *Connected for All Time: Book One* and *Book Two*.

The artwork on the cover is entitled *Angels' Lullaby* and was created by Carolyn Utigard Thomas (www.utigard.com). I'll always remember the spark of joy in my heart when I found this picture of an angel holding a baby. I knew in the moment that the spirit babies had guided me to the perfect image for this book. I want to extend my thanks to Carolyn for allowing me to use this wonderful artwork. Connie Kouba of Kouba Graphics Inc. (www.koubagraphics.com) designed the beautiful cover and did the typesetting for the manuscript. She was a joy to work with and her artistic design abilities brought this project to a delightful conclusion.

This book evolved with the assistance of numerous editors over a period of ten years. My heartfelt thanks to Judith Howard for her countless hours spent editing and formatting this work. Her assistance gave me the creative freedom to write without worrying about the details of grammar, punctuation, and formatting. I also want to thank these editors who contributed to this project at various times: Jan Alligretti, Cynthia Richmond, Jane Francis, Penny Hiernu, Ann Ramage, and Leah Janeczko.

I wish to acknowledge Roy Waite, my mentor and first spiritual teacher. He taught me that spirit communication is real and that, indeed, spirit babies can send messages to their family members here on earth. Thank you also to the numerous healers, psychics, and spiritual mediums who contributed metaphysical insights from their readings: Akeeya, Barbara Norman, Chief Joseph, Sandra Cheek, Carol Tunney, Carol Mann, Jane Francis, Robert Peace, Linda Eastburn, and Wachan, the Inca medicine man.

Finally, I'd like to thank my husband, Dr. Jerry Wesch, for his never-ending support as I fulfilled the call of Spirit to write this book. It's such a joy to have his love and encouragement.

Grief Resources

The organizations listed below provide support and resources for families grieving the loss of a child. In addition, you may want to refer to my website (www.connectedforalltime.com) for a list of spiritual mediums and their contact information.

Bereaved Parents of the USA
Park Forest, Illinois
www.bereavedparents.org

The Compassionate Friends
Oakbrook, Illinois
www.compassionatefriends.org

Forever Family Foundation
Oceanside, New York
www.foreverfamilyfoundation.com

Good Grief Center for Bereavement Support
Pittsburgh, Pennsylvania
www.goodgriefcenter.com

Pregnancy Loss and Infant Death Alliance (PLIDA)
Parker, Colorado
www.plida.org

SHARE Pregnancy and Infant Loss Support
Charles, Missouri
www.nationalshare.org

SIDS Alliance
Baltimore, Maryland
www.sidsalliance.org

National Spiritualist Association of Churches
Lily Dale, New York
www.nsac.org
Provides information about mediums and spiritualist churches

Prayer Wave for After-Death Communication
www.christineduminiak.com
Internet grief support and prayer website
Their mission is to pray for others desiring to receive after-death communication

www.ingramcontent.com/pod-product-compliance
Lightning Source LLC
Chambersburg PA
CBHW070349090426
42733CB00009B/1343